Hi! I'm Cal Croaker.
Join my friends and me as we
explore the weird and wild
world of weather!

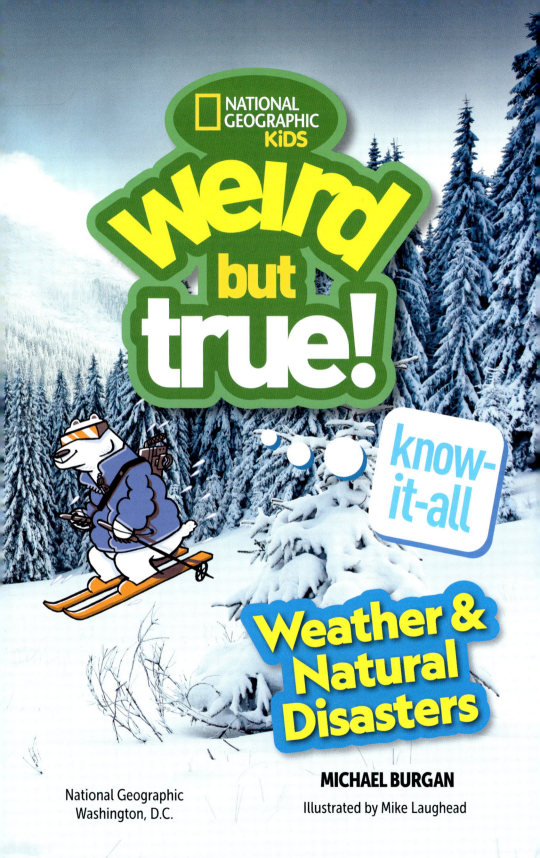

NATIONAL GEOGRAPHIC KiDS

weird but true!

know-it-all

Weather & Natural Disasters

MICHAEL BURGAN

Illustrated by Mike Laughead

National Geographic
Washington, D.C.

CONTENTS

FLOOD AREA

The Wide World of
WEATHER

When you hop out of bed in the morning, one of your first thoughts might be, *What's it like outside?* You can look out a window to see if it's sunny or cloudy, or if trees are swaying in a stiff breeze. If the skies are gray, you might see rain pouring down. If it's cold enough, precipitation might fall as ice or snow. Or maybe you can't see anything at all because fog hides your view.

But wait a minute—what you see outside one minute may not be the same the next. A sunny day can turn stormy quickly, so you might want to check the weather forecast. Specially trained scientists called meteorologists study the atmosphere—the layers of gases that surround Earth—to try to predict how the weather might change. What they say can help you decide if it's a day for shorts, or if you need an umbrella when you head out the door.

CLIMATE TIME

The weather changes day to day and season to season. What the average weather is like in any one part of the world over a long period of time is called that region's climate. You might live in a desert climate, where little rain falls every year.

Around the world, most people live in climates with average land surface temperatures that range between 50 degrees and 86 degrees Fahrenheit (10°–30°C). Some people live in regions with average temperatures that sink down below 32°F (0°C). Humans and wildlife of all kinds can withstand many climate extremes.

In this book, you'll explore what shapes the weather, the main types of climates, and natural disasters that occur when the weather goes wild. You'll also learn about one of the greatest challenges the world faces today: climate change. Around the globe, the atmosphere and the oceans are warming rapidly. That global warming is affecting all life on Earth.

Are you ready to become a weather whiz? Let's dig in!

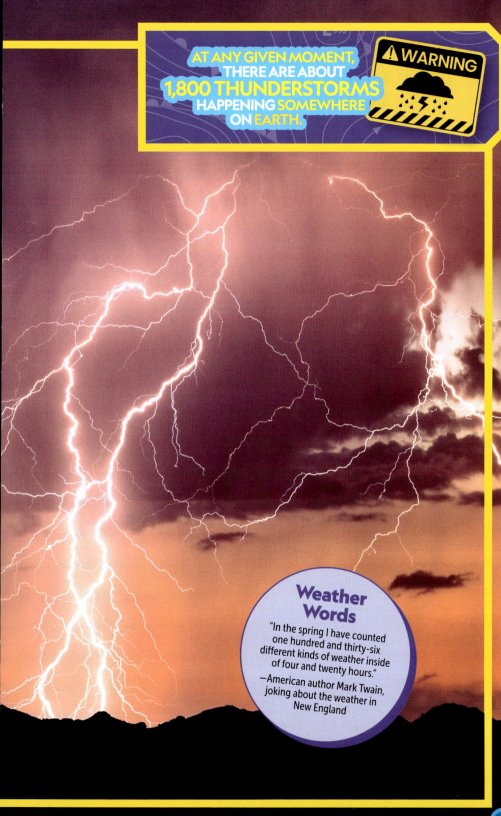

AT ANY GIVEN MOMENT, THERE ARE ABOUT **1,800 THUNDERSTORMS** HAPPENING SOMEWHERE ON EARTH.

⚠ **WARNING**

Weather Words

"In the spring I have counted one hundred and thirty-six different kinds of weather inside of four and twenty hours."

—American author Mark Twain, joking about the weather in New England

Weather
WONDERS

SOME KINDS OF **DUST STORMS**—CALLED **HABOOBS**—CAN BE **100 MILES (160 KM) WIDE.**

RAINDROPS ARE ACTUALLY SHAPED LIKE THE TOP OF A HAMBURGER BUN—THEY HAVE A **FLAT BOTTOM** AND **ROUNDED TOP.**

WEATHER AND **CLIMATE NATURAL DISASTERS** HAVE **COST** THE UNITED STATES MORE THAN **$2.6 TRILLION** SINCE 1980.

>>EVERY YEAR AN ESTIMATED **16 MILLION THUNDERSTORMS** OCCUR AROUND THE WORLD— ABOUT **40,000 PER DAY.**

>>COMMERCIAL AIRPLANES ARE DESIGNED TO WITHSTAND LIGHTNING STRIKES. AN AIRPLANE MAY BE HIT BY LIGHTNING ONCE OR TWICE EACH YEAR!

My record is snow joke!

THE UNITED STATES HAS MORE THAN 1,000 TORNADOES EACH YEAR—MORE THAN ANY OTHER COUNTRY.

>>THE WORLD'S TALLEST SNOWPERSON WAS 122 FEET 1 INCH (37.21 M) TALL.

All Kinds of CLIMATE

On any given day, people in one part of the world might be bundled up against the cold, while others are sweltering in the heat and humidity. What causes the kind of weather they'll face? The climate where they live.

Meteorologists have identified five major climate types:

TROPICAL

HOT ENOUGH FOR YOU? It is if you live in a tropical climate, as in many countries in South America and Africa. These regions have high average temperatures and see heavy rains. You'll learn more about tropical climates on pages 96 to 109.

TEMPERATE

THIS CLIMATE GIVES YOU A LITTLE BIT OF EVERYTHING—summers are warm, winters are mild, and precipitation often falls throughout the year. Large parts of the United States have a temperate climate, as you'll see on pages 118 to 123.

DRY OR ARID

IF YOU'RE PACKING FOR A TRIP TO ONE OF THESE REGIONS, YOU PROBABLY WON'T NEED YOUR RAIN JACKET! Arid regions, such as large parts of Australia, don't get much precipitation. There's more to explore about this climate on pages 112 to 117.

CONTINENTAL

AS IN TEMPERATE REGIONS, SUMMERS CAN BE WARM, BUT WINTERS CAN BE HARSH, with temperatures often dropping into the negative numbers. This type of climate is usually found far from coastal areas and includes a large part of Russia called Siberia. Uncover more continental climate facts starting on page 126.

POLAR

BRRR! **BUNDLE UP WHEN YOU HEAD INTO POLAR CLIMATES,** which are found around Earth's North and South Poles. Average temperatures usually don't go above 50°F (10°C). The northern polar region is called the Arctic, which includes parts of eight nations, including Norway, Sweden, and Finland. Chill out with cool polar facts starting on page 132.

WEATHER HERO: THE CLIMATE GUY

The system we use to describe the major climate types is named for Wladimir Köppen (1846–1940). Born in Russia, this meteorologist outlined five climates based on a region's precipitation, temperature, and the types of plants that thrive in it. Köppen started working on his system during the 1880s and continued to improve it for many years.

That's *Mr. Climate Guy* to you!

SUNNY SKIES!

Enlightening news coming up ...

3NG NEWS

Did You Know?

Without heat from the sun, Earth's average surface temperature would be a very chilly 0°F (−18°C). After a year without that heat, the temperature would plunge to −100°F (−73°C)!

One of the biggest weather wonders is right over your head—about 93 million miles (150 million km) away. That's how far the sun is from Earth. That ball of light is one of billions of trillions of stars in the universe. But that doesn't make it any less special! The sun plays a major role in shaping our daily weather.

HOT STUFF!

The sun is one hot spot. Temperatures on its surface can reach 10,000°F (5500°C), and it's way hotter inside—up to 27 million degrees Fahrenheit (15 million degrees Celsius)!

That's more than 200,000 times hotter than the highest temperature ever recorded on Earth. Energy from the sun, called solar radiation, warms Earth's atmosphere, creating winds and clouds and fueling the water cycle, which gives us precipitation (see page 24).

Some of the sun's energy that reaches Earth is reflected upward. Gases in the atmosphere trap some of that energy and keep it close to Earth. Because of the trapped energy, Earth's average surface temperature is 59°F (15°C).

TILT AND SPIN

Earth's position relative to the sun also affects climate and weather. Earth is tilted a bit on its axis as it circles the sun. This tilt and rotation create the different seasons. When the top half of Earth, the Northern Hemisphere, tilts closer to the sun, that region has its summer. Meanwhile, the Southern Hemisphere is then farther away from the sun, so chilly winter weather sets in. As the year goes on, the seasons in these two hemispheres reverse. Large areas of the two hemispheres also experience spring and fall (autumn).

Earth's tilt and its position around the sun also explain why polar regions are so cold and tropics are so warm. The poles receive the least sunlight compared with other regions, which keeps the temperatures low and gives them just two distinct seasons: summer and winter. The tropics, which are located on either side of the Equator, receive more direct sunlight, so they stay warm throughout the year. The major difference between the seasons in tropical regions is how much rain falls and how cloudy it gets.

SPOT ON

At times, dark spots appear on the sun's surface. These Earth-size spots form when large amounts of magnetic force move from deep within the sun to its surface. When a lot of spots form, the amount of energy the sun produces increases slightly. This could mean a tiny increase in temperatures on Earth over many years, but nothing like the climate change Earth has recently seen. And when sunspots are less common, the planet cools a bit—but not enough for you to notice when you're outdoors.

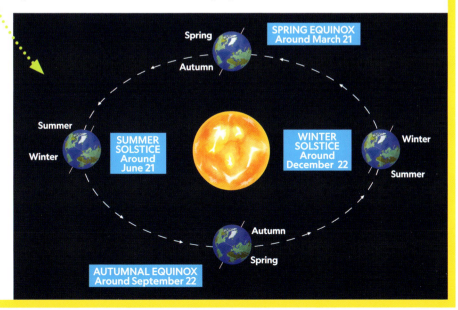

Spring

SPRING EQUINOX
Around March 21

Autumn

Summer

Winter

SUMMER SOLSTICE
Around June 21

WINTER SOLSTICE
Around December 22

Winter

Summer

Autumn

Spring

AUTUMNAL EQUINOX
Around September 22

The Air UP THERE

YOU CAN'T FEEL IT, BUT THE **AIR PRESSING AGAINST YOU** WEIGHS ABOUT **ONE TON** (0.9 T)—THE SAME AS SOME TYPES OF **BUFFALO!**

1 TON

Most weather on Earth occurs in the layer of the atmosphere closest to the planet. This layer, the troposphere, is made up of different gases, which form the air we need to breathe. It's also where clouds develop.

While we couldn't live without the sun's energy, you can get too much of a good thing. The different layers of the atmosphere help shield Earth from receiving too many rays, especially ones that can harm people and other living things. The atmosphere also keeps some heat close to Earth's surface, ensuring life can survive. And even though you can't see or feel the atmosphere, it pushes down on you all the time. This air pressure also plays a role in creating weather.

ON THE MOVE

Heat from the sun causes the air in the atmosphere to move around, creating wind. During daytime, the sun warms the air over land. which heats up and rises, and heavier, cooler air over water moves downward. The reverse happens at night: The air over land cools faster than the air over water. The same kind of movement happens on a global scale, too, as warm air rises over land near the Equator and cold air descends over the North and South Poles. The movement of the warm and cold air creates global wind patterns. You'll learn more about winds on page 84.

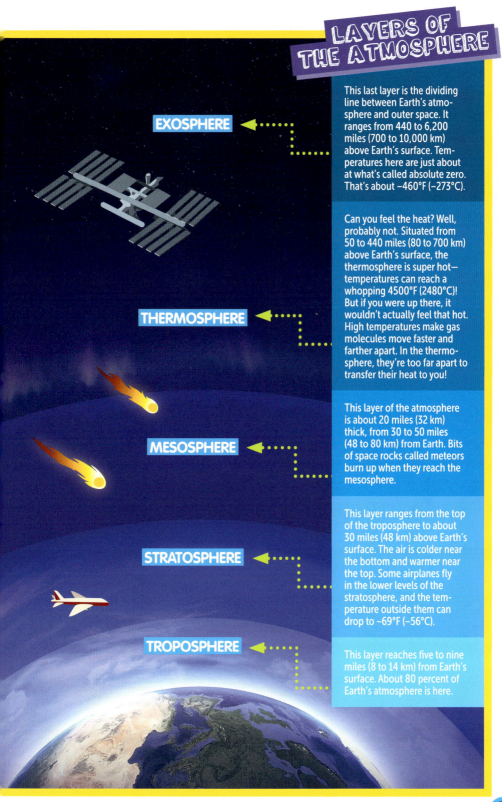

EXOSPHERE

This last layer is the dividing line between Earth's atmosphere and outer space. It ranges from 440 to 6,200 miles (700 to 10,000 km) above Earth's surface. Temperatures here are just about at what's called absolute zero. That's about −460°F (−273°C).

THERMOSPHERE

Can you feel the heat? Well, probably not. Situated from 50 to 440 miles (80 to 700 km) above Earth's surface, the thermosphere is super hot—temperatures can reach a whopping 4500°F (2480°C)! But if you were up there, it wouldn't actually feel that hot. High temperatures make gas molecules move faster and farther apart. In the thermosphere, they're too far apart to transfer their heat to you!

MESOSPHERE

This layer of the atmosphere is about 20 miles (32 km) thick, from 30 to 50 miles (48 to 80 km) from Earth. Bits of space rocks called meteors burn up when they reach the mesosphere.

STRATOSPHERE

This layer ranges from the top of the troposphere to about 30 miles (48 km) above Earth's surface. The air is colder near the bottom and warmer near the top. Some airplanes fly in the lower levels of the stratosphere, and the temperature outside them can drop to −69°F (−56°C).

TROPOSPHERE

This layer reaches five to nine miles (8 to 14 km) from Earth's surface. About 80 percent of Earth's atmosphere is here.

Get Clear
ON CLOUDS

That one's a rabbit ... no, a fox. Have you ever looked up at the clouds and tried to see shapes? Clouds can look like giant, puffy balls of cotton floating across skies of blue. Or they can darken the sky, blocking out the sun. They come in many different types, but they have one thing in common: They are made up of bits of ice and water vapor that cling to dust and other tiny particles in the air. The water and particles form droplets that grow and eventually stick together, forming clouds. When the droplets get really big, they fall to Earth as precipitation.

CUMULONIMBUS

On warm, humid days, winds can push cumulus clouds together high into the sky, creating a cumulonimbus. The top of one can reach more than 30,000 feet (10,000 m), and it can pack a punch! These clouds can unleash powerful thunderstorms and even tornadoes.

STRATUS

Usually found below 6,500 feet (2,000 m), stratus clouds are one of the two main types of low clouds. These clouds are like a thick, gray blanket that blocks out the sun. Some stratus clouds produce steady precipitation.

CUMULUS

Big and puffy, this type of low cloud is common on sunny days. Some people say they look like cotton candy or huge marshmallows!

I'm on cloud nine!

A CUMULUS CLOUD
MAY LOOK LIGHT, BUT IT CAN
WEIGH 1.1 MILLION POUNDS
(500,000 KG)—MORE THAN SIX AVERAGE-SIZE
AIRPLANES PACKED WITH PEOPLE!

CIRRUS

These feathery clouds are the highest of all. They're sometimes called mares' tails because some people think they look like a horse's tail blowing in the breeze. When they float with another kind of cirrus cloud, called cirrocumulus, they can signal a developing storm. Cirrocumulus clouds are made up of smaller "cloudlets" and can look a little like honeycomb or fish scales.

CLOUDS ON OTHER PLANETS

Earth isn't the only planet that has clouds. Most others do, too. Mars has some made of water ice, as Earth does. But some Martian clouds are made of carbon dioxide. On Venus, the clouds contain sulfur dioxide, a gas that smells like fireworks after they've been lit. Saturn and Jupiter have some clouds made of ammonia, while some clouds on Uranus and Neptune are made of methane. And distant planets outside our solar system have clouds made of silicates—the minerals found in sand!

ALTOSTRATUS & ALTOCUMULUS

These clouds look a lot like low-level clouds, but they form higher in the atmosphere, between 6,500 and 20,000 feet (2,000 and 6,000 m). Altostratus clouds sometimes signal that warmer weather or precipitation is on the way.

Rocky WEATHER

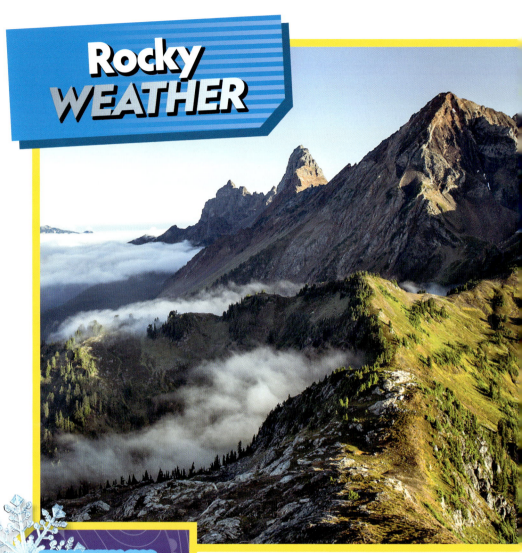

Not everything that affects our weather floats or shines above our heads. Here on Earth, mountains can interact with the air to shape the weather on a peak or on either side of those rocky tops. One side could be as dry as a desert while the other side gets soaked with rain. Here's how mountains affect our weather.

IT'S WINDY UP HERE!

If you've ever hiked up a mountain, you might have noticed that the air feels cooler as you climb. That's because of what happens when wind meets a mountain. When the air meets that mountain barrier, it rises. As it does, it loses some of its water vapor, which is usually in the form of rain or snow. Without the water vapor, the air cools.

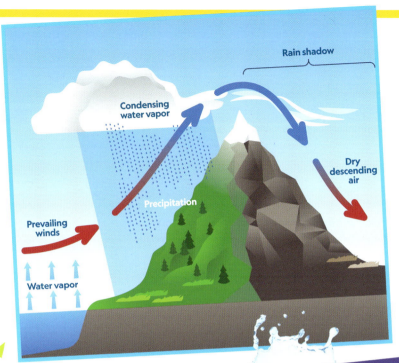

Rain shadow

Condensing
water vapor

Dry
descending
air

Precipitation

Prevailing
winds

Water vapor

A mountaintop can also be windier than the ground below it. Close to the ground, a natural force called friction slows the wind. Trees, shrubs, or even buildings slow the wind, too. But up on a mountain, there are fewer objects to slow the wind. That means the wind comes at you full force, which also makes it feel chillier on top.

MOUNTAIN EXTREMES

Tall mountain ranges can also affect the weather for many miles on either side. Let's take a virtual trip to the Cascade Range in western North America to see how it works. These mountains sit to the east of the Pacific Ocean and include such famous peaks as Mount Rainier and Mount Hood.

Weather systems that form over the ocean can carry lots of water. As these weather systems move inland, most of that moisture falls on the western side and on top of the mountains. As the weather system passes over the mountain, the air begins to fall, warming up as it drops. Any remaining moisture dries up. This process helps explain why the western parts of Washington State get plenty of rain and snow, while some regions east of the mountains are deserts.

WEATHER WONDERS: AS WET AS IT GETS

If you visit Wai'ale'ale on the Hawaiian island of Kaua'i, be prepared to get drenched! Just over 5,100 feet (1,554 m) high, this mountain is the rainiest spot in the United States and among the wettest spots on the entire planet. During an average year, about 30 feet (9 m) of rain falls on the mountain. You'd need a bucket taller than some telephone poles to collect that much water!

Hot SPOTS

Pardon the eruption, er, I mean interruption.

CLOUDS OF SMOKE AND ASH FROM A VOLCANIC ERUPTION

One kind of mountain can cause some really big weather disruptions. When volcanoes erupt, they spew a steamy stew of melted rock, minerals, and gases that can reach more than 2000°F (1090°C). But believe it or not, some of that hot stuff can actually make parts of Earth chill out. Let's find out how.

A BLAST OF GAS AND ASH

A volcanic eruption sends gases, ash, and dust into the atmosphere—up to 28 miles (45 km) high. One of the gases, sulfur dioxide, merges with water in the air and becomes tiny droplets of a liquid called sulfuric acid. The acid can float through the atmosphere for up to three years and drift far from the volcano that produced it. In the air,

AN ERUPTION OF THE KARYMSKY VOLCANO, KAMCHATKA PENINSULA, RUSSIA

the acid reflects some of the sun's energy away from Earth. This can lead to small drops in temperature.

One example from centuries ago shows the effects of sulfuric acid on the weather. The eruption of a volcano in Laki, Iceland, in 1783 went on for months and had a devastating effect. It unleashed a cloud of sulfur dioxide and ash that weighed an estimated 120 million tons (109 million t). Acid rain destroyed crops, which led many people to starve. The cloud of gas and ash reached North America, where average temperatures fell about 1.8°F (1°C) across the continent.

WARMING THINGS UP

While some volcanic clouds have a quick cooling effect, they might also play a role in heating things up. Some of the gas in the cloud is carbon dioxide (CO_2). This is one of the greenhouse gases that is causing global warming (see page 144). The amount of CO_2 in a volcanic eruption is tiny compared to what humans create by burning oil, coal, and gas. Large eruptions probably release enough CO_2 to warm the planet, but only slightly.

IN 1991, A **VOLCANIC BLAST** FROM MOUNT PINATUBO IN THE PHILIPPINES **COOLED TEMPERATURES** AROUND THE WORLD BY AS MUCH AS **1.3°F** (.72°C).

REALLY OLD RAIN

An ancient volcanic eruption has helped scientists learn more about Earth's early atmosphere. About 2.7 billion years ago, a volcano erupted in what is today South Africa. Soon after, rain fell on some of the volcanic ash on the ground, then more ash covered the tiny holes the raindrops had created. Over time, all the ash turned to stone, leaving a record of the raindrops' impact. The scientists could tell the size of the drops by the size of the holes they made. The air pressure determined the speed and size of the drops. By comparing those ancient raindrop holes with ones made by rain that falls today, scientists learned that ancient air pressure was not much different from today's. But ancient Earth's atmosphere likely contained a lot of strong greenhouse gases, which helped keep the planet warm at a time when the sun's energy was not as powerful.

Weather
MYTHS

For thousands of years, people have tried to explain what causes weather with tall tales and creative theories. Today, meteorologists know a lot of these ideas just aren't true. Here's a look at some of the world's weather myths and stories.

THOR AND THUNDER

The Norse believed their god Thor was the source of thunder. The hammer-holding god was said to zoom across the heavens in a chariot pulled by goats, causing the rumbling heard on Earth. He was also said to cause lightning when he threw his hammer at enemies.

GREEK GODS OF THE WINDS

In Greek mythology, the gods were said to cause all kinds of weather. Zeus, king of the gods, hurled lightning bolts at his enemies. Different gods were also said to summon the winds that blew in the four directions—east, west, north, and south. Zephyr was the god of the west wind, and that word is still used today to describe a gentle breeze.

TLÁLOC AND THE RAINS

To the Aztec of what is today Mexico, the god Tláloc was a lifesaver. Tláloc brought rains that helped crops grow. But make him mad and he would stop the rain, which caused crop-killing droughts.

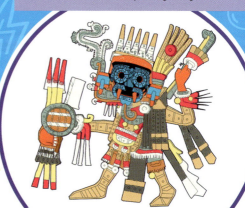

TRY TO FRY

When it's really hot, some people say you can fry an egg on the sidewalk. Well, not *eggs*-xactly. In most cases, an egg wouldn't heat up enough to cook it all the way through. That takes a temperature of 158°F (70°C). Most sidewalks, even in really hot weather, would only reach 145°F (63°C).

YUKI-ONNA'S BREATH OF DEATH

If you lived in ancient Japan, you didn't want to anger a female spirit called a *yuki-onna*. The name means "snow woman," and a yuki-onna could do more than give people the cold shoulder—she could freeze them to death with her breath!

A RAINY MOO-MENT?

Myths about the weather still swirl around today. Some people believe that cows can predict the weather: They lie down in their fields when rain is on the way. But cows stretch out on the ground for a lot of reasons, and there's no proof that approaching rain is one of them.

FORECASTER PHIL?

Better keep that sweater handy!

In Punxsutawney, Pennsylvania, U.S.A., a groundhog named Phil is the star of Groundhog Day every year on February 2. The story goes that if Phil pops out of his winter hibernation hole and sees his shadow, winter weather will last for another six weeks. No shadow means an early spring is on the way. Phil's holiday has its roots in old European folklore, but his weather prediction skills are not on totally solid ground. Since 1969, Phil has only been right about one of every three winters.

Water WORKS

About 71 percent of Earth's surface is covered with water. You can't always see it, but some of that water is constantly on the move. The sun helps power what's called the water cycle. This cycle can't take you anywhere, but it does help make all life on Earth possible. And this cycle also recycles—rain that falls on you today has been around for almost four billion years!

During its travels through the cycle, water can be a solid, a liquid, or a gas. Here are the major parts of the water cycle.

CONDENSATION

As water vapor floats toward the sky, it begins to cool. Then it teams up with the dust and other tiny particles floating in the atmosphere. This forms clouds, which eventually release precipitation, and the water cycle begins again.

EVAPORATION

The sun's warming energy turns water on Earth's surface into water vapor that rises to the sky. The heat from the sun breaks the bonds that keep water molecules close together. With that break, water changes from a liquid to a gas. Plants also release water vapor after they absorb water from the soil. This process is called transpiration.

THANKS TO THE WATER CYCLE, THE **WATER** YOU DRINK IS THE SAME WATER THAT **DINOSAURS DRANK!**

PRECIPITATION

Clouds are made up of water vapor that clings to tiny particles in the air (see page 16). When the droplets they form are heavy enough, they fall to the ground as rain or snow.

COLLECTION

Whether it's rain or snow, precipitation collects somewhere on Earth. Some rain falls directly into streams, lakes, and oceans. Some enters the ground. Ice and snow can collect on land or form glaciers. When the temperature is warm enough, the ice and snow melt and flow into rivers and streams or directly into the ground.

Awesome Facts
ABOUT RAIN

Rain, rain, go away ... We might not want it to rain on our parade or other outdoor events, but rain is an important part of the water cycle. It often starts out as snow or ice when it first falls from the clouds, then turns to liquid as it passes through warm parts of the atmosphere. Here's a look at some fun facts about the wet stuff.

HIGH AND DRY

Want to stay drier when it starts to rain? It might be better to take a sprint through the downpour. The number of drops that pelt your head in a second is the same, whether you walk or run through the rain. But some researchers think your total time spent in the rain plays a role in how wet you'll be. If you are trying to move from one point to another, going faster generally means you'll spend less time in the rain, which means you'll likely reduce the total number of drops that hit you. Other factors like wind and direction of the rain also play a role, though, so it's hard to say for certain whether you should walk or run.

DISAPPEARING RAIN

Sometimes, you can see what looks like thin tails hanging from clouds in the distance. Those wisps are called virga, and they're actually raindrops that evaporate in drier parts of the atmosphere before they hit the ground.

TAKING SHAPE

Raindrops are often said to look like teardrops or pears. But as they form, they're more like tiny balls, then they flatten out as they get closer to the ground. A video from NASA, the U.S. space agency, showed that as drops move through the air, they look more like the top half of a hamburger bun!

BURNING RAIN

Not all rain is good for plants and other life on Earth. Some rain forms as water vapor that clings to particles of harmful gases called sulfur dioxide and nitrogen oxides. These gases are part of the pollution produced by factories and motor vehicles. The water vapor and the gases create acid rain, which can kill fish and other creatures in streams and lakes, along with plants and trees. The good news is, governments have passed laws that help reduce air pollution and lower the amount of these harmful gases in the atmosphere, reducing the amount of acid rain.

BY THE NUMBERS

RECORD RAINS

Most rain in 24 hours in the United States:
49.69 inches (126.2 cm), Waipā Garden, Kaua'i, Hawaii (2018)

Most rain in 24 hours in the world:
71.8 inches (182.5 cm), Foc-Foc, Réunion Island (1966)

Most rain in one minute:
1.23 inches (3.12 cm), Unionville, Maryland, U.S.A. (1956)

Most rain in one hour:
12 inches (30.5 cm), Holt, Missouri, U.S.A. (1947)

Most rain over a 12-month period:
1,042 inches (26.47 m), Cherrapunji, India (August 1860–July 1861)

Smells like rain!

WEATHER HERO: ON THE NOSE

When rain falls after a dry spell, it sometimes has its own smell. That aroma is called petrichor, and an Australian chemist named Isabel "Joy" Bear (1927–2021) helped identify what causes it. When the weather is hot and dry, certain rocks release an oil. That oil combines with rain to create the smell.

Furious FLOODS

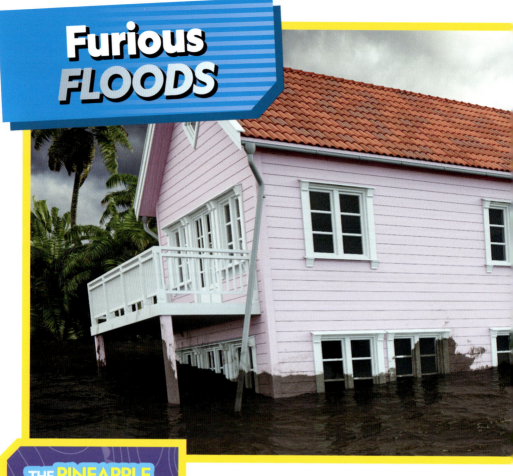

Aloha!

ain is essential for life on Earth, but when rain falls for too long or too quickly in one area, it can cause flooding. Rivers flow over their banks, and the rushing waters can destroy buildings and carry away cars.

Periods of extreme rain can also cause mudslides. The ground can absorb rain, but when it comes too quickly, the water mixes with the soil on the surface and turns to mud. That mud can then slide downhill, and, like a flood, carry away anything in its path.

RIVERS OF RAIN

Some extreme rain events are caused by atmospheric rivers. You can't cross these rivers with a bridge. They are in the air above us. Strong winds carry long columns of moisture from tropical ocean regions over land. These rivers of rain can be more than 1,200 miles (1,900 km) long and 300 miles (480 km) wide.

Some atmospheric rivers can bring needed rain to parched lands. And in the winter, the rivers bring snow to

some mountains. The snow eventually melts, providing farmers with water. But when the winds stall and the rivers drop a lot of rain in one area, flooding occurs. During the winter of 2022–23, parts of the U.S. state of California were hit with a series of atmospheric rivers. Some areas were drenched with two or three times their usual rainfall. The record rains washed out roads and knocked out power.

A SATELLITE IMAGE OF THE ATMOSPHERIC RIVER CALLED THE PINEAPPLE EXPRESS

WAYBACK WEATHER: FEARSOME FLOODS

Some of the worst flooding in world history has taken place in China along the Huang, or Yellow, River. In 1887, flooding stretched out over several months, as heavy rains fell and dams burst. Flood-water covered approximately 5,800 square miles (15,000 sq km) of land—an area bigger than the U.S. state of Connecticut. The rising waters and diseases the floodwaters helped spread killed at least one million people. Today, a dam 505 feet (154 m) high and 4,321 feet (1,317 m) long is meant to help control flooding along the river.

Johnstown,
Pennsylvania, U.S.A.

THE FLOOD WAS POWERFUL ENOUGH TO CARRY TRAIN LOCOMOTIVES THAT WEIGHED 85 TONS (77 T) ALMOST ONE MILE (1.6 KM).

For weeks during spring 1889, heavy rains fell around Johnstown, Pennsylvania, U.S.A. Then, a powerful storm hit the state on May 30, and rivers began to rise. In the town of Coburn, floodwaters rose almost 11 feet (3.5 m) in just 30 minutes. But the worst effects of the "Great Storm" were still to come.

A DAMAGED DAM

In Johnstown, the waters of Lake Conemaugh crept upward, too. A dam on the lake had a spillway, where rising waters could pass through. But the storm had carried trees and logs into the lake, clogging the spillway. On May 31, the lake's waters rose over the dam, and then, horrifyingly, the dam itself gave way. Twenty million tons (18.1 million t) of water rushed and rumbled straight toward the town center. The flood carried away buildings, bridges, animals, and people, creating a devastating humanitarian crisis.

A DARING RESCUE

Caught up in the giant wave of water was six-year-old Gertrude Quinn. She clung to a mattress as the flood carried her along. Bits of debris bumped and bounced off her soggy "raft." She saw a group of people on a roof that had ripped off its building and was now floating in the water. A man named Maxwell McAchren dove off the roof and fought through the raging waters to rescue Gertrude. She clung to his neck as they drifted along, until they came to the top of a small white building. At a window inside, two men stood with poles for people in the floodwaters to grab. McAchren and Gertrude were too far out to reach the poles, but McAchren was able to toss the girl to the men, and to safety.

McAchren survived the flood, too, but many others were not so lucky. The Johnstown Flood killed more than 2,200 people, and hundreds more went missing. Large parts of the town were completely destroyed. But people across the United States and from other countries soon sent more than three million dollars (worth more than $97 million today) to help the survivors and to rebuild the town.

You can count on us!

HELPING HANDS

One group that helped the survivors of the flood was the American Red Cross. The organization had been started eight years before by a nurse named Clara Barton. She and other Red Cross workers reached Johnstown just days after the flood. This marked the first time the American Red Cross helped survivors of a natural disaster, and the group still comes to the rescue today.

Did You Know?

The floodwater and debris it carried formed a wave estimated to be 40 feet (12 m) high and a half-mile (805 m) wide. That's as tall as a four-story building.

Colors Across THE SKY

I agree! Rainbows are very *moo*-ving.

A rainy day can wrap up with a bow on it—a rainbow, that is. When conditions are just right, you can see this colorful, curved arc bending across the sky. What you see is really only part of a full circle of colors. The ground blocks our view of the rest of the circle. But from an airplane, in just the right spot, passengers have seen that full circle.

THE LIGHT STUFF

A rainbow is what's called an optical illusion. It's not something you can touch. We only see them because sunlight passes through water droplets at just the right angle. The

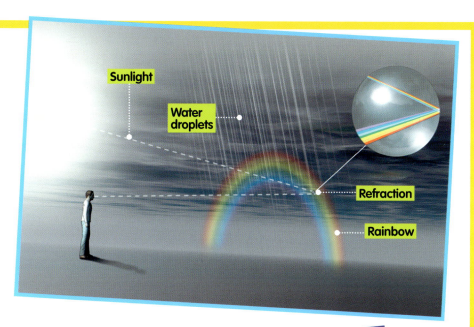

Sunlight

Water droplets

Refraction

Rainbow

position of the sun and where you're standing play a part in whether you can see a rainbow.

But where do the colors come from? The light our eyes can detect is made up of wavelengths of energy. Different waves have different lengths, which our eyes see as the seven colors of the rainbow: red, orange, yellow, green, blue, indigo, and violet. In a rainbow, these colors always appear in this same order, from top to bottom.

BOUNCING AND BENDING

To see a rainbow, you usually need the sun at your back and water droplets in the air in front of you. When sunlight enters a drop, the light bends just slightly—this is called refraction. The bending of the light separates it into the seven different wavelengths of color. These wavelengths then reflect off the back of the drop and scoot out the front, where they're refracted again and form the rainbow we can see.

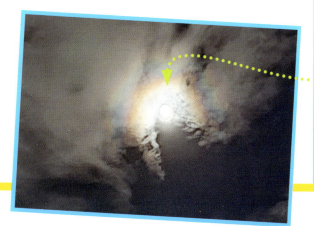

OTHER BOW SHOWS

Double rainbow:
A second, faint rainbow sometimes forms above the main one when light is reflected twice inside the water droplets. The order of colors in the second rainbow is the reverse of the main rainbow.

Fogbow:
Fog is made up of water droplets, so they can refract and reflect light, too. But the drops are smaller than the ones that form rainbows, so fogbows are not as colorful.

Moonbow:
The moon reflects sunlight toward Earth, and that light can create bows, too. But because the moon's light is not very strong, moonbows usually appear as faint rings of colored light around the moon.

Stormy WEATHER

Thunder can give you an idea of the distance between you and a lightning bolt. After you see a flash of lightning, count the seconds that pass before you hear thunder. If it takes five seconds, the lightning is about one mile (1.6 km) away. If the thunder comes after just one second, the lightning is only about 1,000 feet (305 m) away!

oom! Thunderstorms can rattle your house with ground-shaking rumbles and light up the sky with startling bolts of electricity. (You'll learn more about lightning on page 36.)

Most thunderstorms only cover a small area, forming a circle about 15 miles (24 km) wide. A typical storm pops up pretty quickly and then moves on after just 30 minutes. But thunderstorms can really pack a punch in that short time span. They can unleash damaging winds, heavy rain that leads to flash floods, and even hail or tornadoes. And the biggest, strongest storms can last several hours. Here's how they work.

A STORM FORMS

So what are thunderstorms exactly? Thunderstorms are a stew of rising warm air, cool air, and moisture. The warm air carries moisture, which starts to form into a tall cumulus cloud called a cell. As more moisture rises, the cloud grows taller. Cooler air in the atmosphere creates what's called a downdraft, which sends the precipitation rushing down toward Earth.

The warm air that makes a thunderstorm form can get a boost skyward in different ways. Sometimes the air flows upward along mountains and toward the sky. Other times, thunderstorms form when a warm front and a cold front collide (see more about weather fronts on page 71). But even the heat of a summer day can warm the air enough to push it upward to form a storm cloud. That's why you might notice more storms during the summer months in certain parts of the world.

THUNDEROUS "APPLAUSE"

And what about the rumbling noise that gives these storms their name? Thunder happens as lightning bolts travel through the air—the bolts heat the air around them, and then almost immediately, the air cools and contracts. This rapid change creates loud, and sometimes startling, waves of sound.

I call this look stormy chic!

SOME **WINDS** IN A **THUNDERSTORM**, CALLED STRAIGHT LINE WINDS, CAN REACH SPEEDS OF **100 MILES AN HOUR** (160 KM/H).

THREE STAGES OF A THUNDERSTORM

Developing:
During this stage air pushes up (called an updraft) through the cumulus cloud, causing it to grow taller. This lasts about 10 minutes, and there is usually little or no rain but maybe some lightning.

Mature:
During this stage, air is still pushing up at the same time that precipitation is moving down (called a downdraft) and then out of the cloud. This stage lasts about 20 minutes and is peak time for heavy rain, strong winds, and possibly tornadoes.

Dissipating:
Eventually, the downdraft created by the precipitation causes the updraft to fizzle out and the storm subsides. Lightning, though, can still be a threat during this stage.

Mighty LIGHTNING

ONE LIGHTNING BOLT CAN **HEAT** THE **AIR** AROUND IT TO 50,000°F (27,760°C)—**FIVE TIMES HOTTER** THAN THE SURFACE OF THE SUN.

Bacon and eggs, mac and cheese, peanut butter and jelly—some things on your plate just go together. In the weather world, one famous pair is thunder and lightning. Every thunderstorm has bolts from above—hot flashes of electricity that light up the sky. But why does lightning occur? Here's how these bolts behave.

POSITIVELY ELECTRIC

When thunderclouds form, ice crystals crash together. These collisions release tiny particles with electrical charges. Some particles have negative charges, others have positive charges. The electrical energy between the positive and negative charges builds and builds ... until ... flash! It produces a bolt of lightning.

Another kind of lightning, called cloud-to-ground, forms between negative charges in the bottom of the cloud and positive electrical charges in objects on the ground. These objects include trees, which is why you shouldn't stand under one during a thunderstorm! These lightning strikes are the ones we usually see—and the ones that can cause damage with their electrical energy.

HOT BOLT

COLD BOLT

HOT AND COLD BOLTS

You might be surprised to learn that lightning isn't something that only happens during thunderstorms. It can form over erupting volcanoes, too. High winds from the volcano create crashing particles above the volcano. This leads to the same negative and positive charges found in thunderclouds, which can lead to lightning. Intense forest fires can also spark lightning, as they can create clouds similar to thunderclouds. The lightning caused by fires can sometimes spark more fires.

Winter weather can bring lightning, too. During some snowstorms, thunderclouds can form and produce lightning in the same way they do during summer storms. But the winter storms don't produce as much lightning because of the colder temperatures. This "thundersnow" happens mostly with storms that drop six inches (15 cm) or more of snow over 24 hours.

WEATHER HERO: BEN'S BRIGHT IDEA

This weather is *electric*-fying!

Benjamin Franklin (1706–1790) was an American statesman, scientist, and inventor. In 1752, he wanted to prove that lightning was a form of electricity. Franklin flew a kite during a thunderstorm. Electricity in the air from the storm sent a charge through a wire at the top of the kite, down the kite string, and into a metal key near Franklin's hand. He got a shock when he touched the key, proving his theory.

TORNADO WARNING!

No time for funny business, tornadoes are serious.

3NG NEWS

Did You Know?

A rare outbreak of December tornadoes struck eight U.S. states in 2021, with more than 60 hitting in just 24 hours.

You've already learned that when masses of warm and cold air collide, they can form cells, which create thunderstorms. Sometimes, these collisions can create superpowerful thunderstorms called supercells. In these, swirling winds in the clouds pick up speed and form a spinning column that moves down to the ground in a vortex, or funnel. The winds at the ground can reach up to 300 miles an hour (483 km/h). Not all tornadoes come from supercells, but the most powerful ones often do.

More tornadoes form and reach land in North America than on any other continent—about 1,000 touch down every year. Most occur during the summer, when thunderstorms are more likely to form. But tornadoes have been recorded on every continent except icy Antarctica. It lacks the warm, moist air needed to create a tornado. However, the deadliest twister ever recorded roared through the Asian nation of Bangladesh in 1989. That tornado was a mile (1.6 km) wide and traveled for 10 miles (16 km). It wiped out all the buildings over an area of several miles and killed or injured thousands of people.

A TWIST ON TORNADOES

Rating	Wind Speed	Damage
EF0	65–85 mph 105–137 km/h	minor roof, branches
EF1	86–110 mph 138–177 km/h	broken windows
EF2	111–135 mph 178–217 km/h	roofs off, large trees
EF3	136–165 mph 218–266 km/h	homes damaged
EF4	166–200 mph 267–322 km/h	homes leveled
EF5	200+ mph 322+ km/h	incredible damage

TORNADO RATING

So Dusty

Not all tornadoes form in thunderstorms. Similar funnel-shaped clouds can form over dry, dusty land. Called dust devils, these little twisters start with warm air rising up from the ground. At times, the air forms a column that sucks up more warm air and then dirt from the ground. Most dust devils are small and don't last long, but the deserts of Arizona, U.S.A., can spark ones that can last for an hour or more.

Watery Whirlwinds

Some twisters whip up over water. These waterspouts start when supercells move over open waters. Less powerful versions can also form without the presence of supercells. Warm ocean air and moisture moving up to the sky can create a vortex.

TORNADOES DON'T TEND TO LAST LONG. A TYPICAL TWISTER LASTS LESS THAN 10 MINUTES.

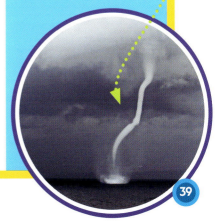

Terrible
TORNADOES

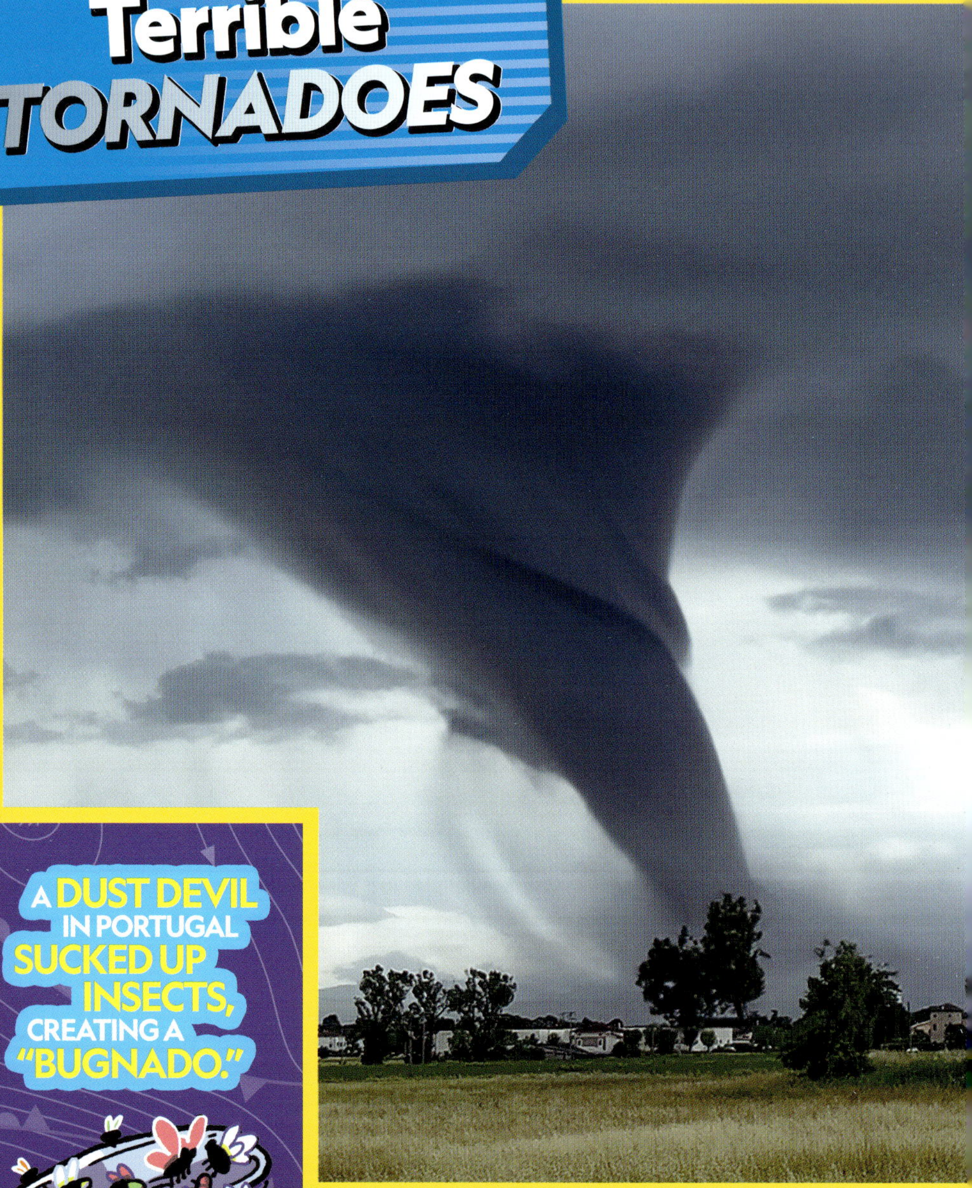

Wheeee!

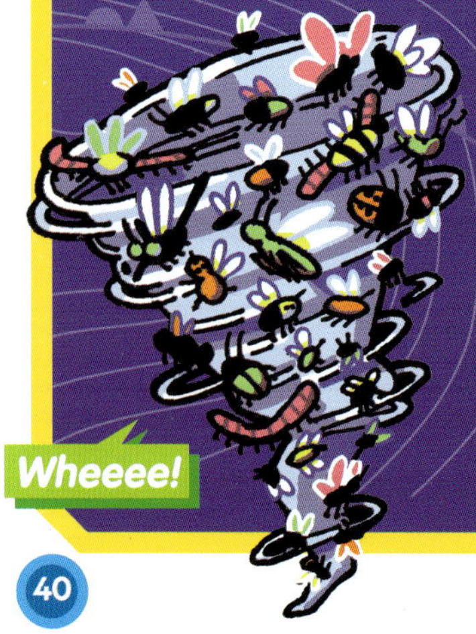

Tornadoes have been known to lift cars and trucks and carry them for hundreds of feet. Smaller items might sail through the skies for up to 150 miles (241 km). The high winds can also turn everyday items, like window glass or pieces of wood, into deadly missiles. Even something soft and lightweight, like a piece of straw or hay, has been known to pierce a much harder object, like a brick, because of the incredible speed at which the lighter

item was traveling. Or, as happened in Texas, U.S.A., in 2015, things planted firmly in the ground, like corn crops, can be carried high into the air. During this event, ice in the clouds covered the corn stalks, which then fell back to Earth as corny "hail."

A tornado gets its carrying power from spinning winds. These winds create an updraft, which sucks up objects of all sizes. Unlike the winds from other storms, which move along the ground, a tornado's winds move up and down. This vertical movement propels objects into the air, sometimes for as long as the tornado keeps spinning. The objects move with the twister.

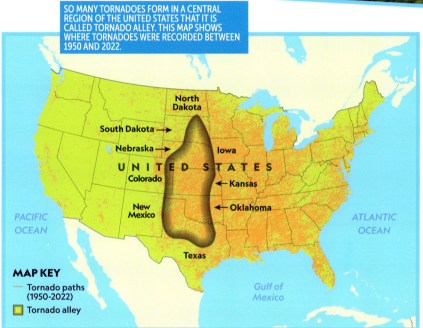

SO MANY TORNADOES FORM IN A CENTRAL REGION OF THE UNITED STATES THAT IT IS CALLED TORNADO ALLEY. THIS MAP SHOWS WHERE TORNADOES WERE RECORDED BETWEEN 1950 AND 2022.

North Dakota
South Dakota →
Nebraska →
Iowa
UNITED STATES
Colorado
← Kansas
New Mexico
← Oklahoma
PACIFIC OCEAN
ATLANTIC OCEAN
Texas
Gulf of Mexico

MAP KEY
— Tornado paths (1950-2022)
■ Tornado alley

WAYBACK WEATHER: THE TRI-STATE TWISTER

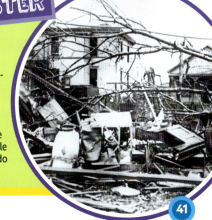

On March 18, 1925, residents of the U.S. states of Missouri, Illinois, and Indiana had no warning when a supercell dropped down a powerful tornado. Traveling at a speed of more than 60 miles an hour (97 km/h), with winds estimated to be more than 300 miles an hour (483 km/h), the funnel cloud ripped through the three states. It carved a path 219 miles (352 km) long—about the distance from New York to Boston—and up to one mile (1.6 km) wide. This tri-state twister became the deadliest in U.S. history. It killed at least 695 people and destroyed 15,000 homes. Some scientists think the deadly tornado may have actually been several tornadoes on the same path.

Race TO CHASE

RESEARCHERS CHASE A SEVERE STORM IN NEBRASKA, U.S.A.

HOWARD BLUESTEIN

Weather Words

"Tornadoes are very difficult to study because it's so hard to make measurements—they don't last long, they encompass a small area, and they're difficult to predict."

—Howard Bluestein

When meteorologists message that a supercell has the potential to unleash a tornado, warning signals might blare, telling people to head for shelter. But instead of running away from twisters, some people chase after them. Who are these daredevils who race toward tornadoes?

IN THE NAME OF SCIENCE

Many storm chasers are scientists looking to gather information about tornadoes—how they form, where they might form, and how they move. The data, the tornado experts hope, could help meteorologists give people more time to prepare before a tornado strikes. The information collected could also help people design buildings that can withstand the swirling winds.

Howard Bluestein is one of these scientific storm chasers. For several decades, he's chased tornadoes in Oklahoma, which is in the heart of Tornado Alley. He was the first scientist to measure winds that reached 280 miles an hour (450 km/h)—the first time a tornado was officially measured to hit EF5 on the Enhanced Fujita Scale. Bluestein got within one mile (1.6 km) of that powerful twister—close enough to see a house bounce in front of him!

That close call shows how dangerous storm chasing can be. The highly respected tornado chaser Tim Samaras died in 2013 when a tornado destroyed the car he was in. During his career, Samaras became known for designing tools that helped measure what was happening inside a tornado.

A PROFESSIONAL STORM CHASER WITH HIS GEAR

TOOLS OF THE TORNADO TRADE

One of Samaras's inventions was nicknamed "the turtle." Its cone-shaped top looks a little like a turtle's shell. The turtle could survive winds of more than 200 miles an hour (322 km/h) to measure the wind speed and direction, air pressure, and humidity inside a twister.

Other tools used to detect and measure tornadoes include a form of radar called Doppler (see page 72) and light detection and ranging (LiDAR) systems. As the name suggests, LiDAR tracks storms with light, in the form of a laser. The laser can measure how quickly tiny particles move near a storm, helping to measure wind speed.

AMATEUR HOUR

Not all storm chasers are scientists. Some chasers race after tornadoes trying to film them, and perhaps they like the thrill of being so close to such a powerful force of nature. But officials warn that these amateurs block roads and impede traffic, including emergency vehicles.

WARNING TORNADO !

STORM SPOTTERS

Storm chasing is best left to the experts. But just about anyone can learn to be a storm spotter, as part of SKYWARN. The National Weather Service (NWS) of the United States relies on several hundred thousand SKYWARN volunteers to watch for severe thunderstorms and other weather hazards. The spotters pass on information to NWS and local officials, which can help them prepare for storms.

SURVIVOR STORIES:
WHAT A TRIP!

Ⓘn March 2006, Matt Suter heard reports that a tornado was approaching his grandmother's mobile home in Fordland, Missouri, U.S.A. He ignored warnings to take shelter. Suddenly, winds of more than 100 miles an hour (161 km/h) broke a window, and Matt felt the twister rock the trailer. That was the last thing he remembered, as a lamp rocketed into his head, knocking him out cold. He missed what turned out to be the ride of a lifetime!

When he finally woke up, Matt was lying in a field more than 1,300 feet (400 m) away from where the trailer had been—almost the length of four football fields placed end to end. Amazingly, his only injuries were a bump and cut from the lamp and scratches on his feet. Matt wasn't the first person to be sucked up and flung by a tornado. But he set a record for traveling the farthest under twister power.

ARCTIC OCEAN

NORTH AMERICA
EUROPE
ASIA
● Fordland, Missouri, U.S.A.
PACIFIC OCEAN
AFRICA
PACIFIC OCEAN
SOUTH AMERICA
INDIAN OCEAN
AUSTRALIA
ATLANTIC OCEAN
SOUTHERN OCEAN
ANTARCTICA

THE INSIDE SCOOP

The odds of being picked up and carried by a tornado are pretty slim, unless you're a storm chaser. And you should always listen to warnings when a tornado is nearby. But if you could see inside a tornado, you'd spot everything else the swirling winds had sucked up. This would likely include trees and pieces of buildings destroyed by the tornado. The powerful winds also create deafening noises, like the sound of a jet engine starting. Some of the sounds are infrasounds, meaning they're too low for humans to hear, though some birds and other animals can detect them.

It would be hard to breathe inside a tornado. The air inside and near the bottom of a tornado has much less pressure than the air outside it. It's hard to breathe where the air pressure is lower—like up high on a mountain—because the air has less oxygen in it.

HIGH FLIERS

HERE ARE SOME OF THE ANIMALS (THEY SURVIVED!) AND OBJECTS THAT HAVE BEEN CARRIED AWAY BY TORNADOES IN THE U.S.

2017
A weak tornado that hit Elgin, Texas, was said to still be strong enough to pick up several cows.

2011
A car traveled half a mile (0.8 km) when it was picked up by an EF5 tornado that struck Smithville, Mississippi.

1955
A horse owned by a family in Bowdle, South Dakota, flew 1,000 feet (305 m) and landed in a ditch.

1954
An EF4 tornado that struck Worcester, Massachusetts, carried a wedding dress up to 100 miles (161 km) away.

1915
A tornado that hit Kansas carried a canceled check more than 200 miles (322 km) to Palmyra, Nebraska.

1887
A New York newspaper reported that a water-spout—a tornado over water—picked up an alligator and dropped it on land.

Tornado-Chasing *PRO*

Did You Know?

Professional storm chasers usually drive armored trucks to help protect them from a tornado's power.

ANTON SEIMON

A TORNADO FORMS IN EL RENO, OKLAHOMA, U.S.A., ON MAY 31, 2013.

THIS WEATHER VAN DROVE VERY CLOSE TO THE EL RENO TORNADO—THE LARGEST TORNADO IN HISTORY.

In the world of storm chasers, Anton Seimon is a top tornado tracker. He is a meteorologist and geographer, and one of National Geographic's Explorers—experts in many fields working around the globe. Seimon's research of more than 30 years keeps him in motion, chasing twisters up and down Tornado Alley.

Seimon worked with famed storm chaser Tim Samaras (see page 43) on a project that featured a device called Tinman. It held one video camera and three photo cameras meant to take images inside a tornado. Seimon, Samaras, and their team traveled 50,000 miles (80,467 km) during three spring seasons, trying to get this inside info and learn more about twisters. They only managed a few shots with one camera before Tinman met its end, crushed by powerful winds. But the work was worth it—Tinman had shot the first pictures ever taken right next to a powerful funnel.

THE EL RENO SURVEY

Anton Seimon also started the El Reno Survey. Working with several other scientists, they studied the El Reno tornado of 2013 (see sidebar). The project was unique because the team used crowdsourcing—they reached out to all storm chasers using social media—to study and tell the story of the storm by gathering as much photo and video imagery as possible.

Using software they developed, the El Reno Survey then linked the different images with maps and radar data. That created a three-dimensional view of the tornado as it moved—the first time scientists had this kind of information.

THE EL RENO TORNADO

The tornado that formed in El Reno, Oklahoma, U.S.A., on May 31, 2013, was one for the record books. At 2.6 miles (4.2 km), it was the widest tornado ever recorded, and its winds reached 300 miles an hour (483 km/h), some of the fastest winds ever measured. It was, at the time, perhaps the best documented tornado by storm chasers. As many as 300 teams of chasers were on the scene that day. The tornado also released smaller tornadoes from inside it, called secondary or sub-vortices. In El Reno, these mini-twisters packed the most powerful winds. Sadly, it was a sub-vortex that killed Tim Samaras, his son Paul, and Carl Young, their teammate.

Tropical PUNCH

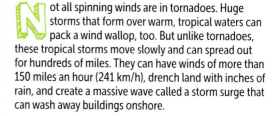

Not all spinning winds are in tornadoes. Huge storms that form over warm, tropical waters can pack a wind wallop, too. But unlike tornadoes, these tropical storms move slowly and can spread out for hundreds of miles. They can have winds of more than 150 miles an hour (241 km/h), drench land with inches of rain, and create a massive wave called a storm surge that can wash away buildings onshore.

WHAT'S IN A NAME?

Depending on where they form, strong tropical storms are referred to as hurricanes, cyclones, or typhoons. Ones that develop in the North Atlantic, central North Pacific, and eastern North Pacific Oceans are called hurricanes. They're called cyclones when they form over the South Pacific and Indian Oceans, and typhoons when they develop in the Northwest Pacific.

THE GROWING STORM

Whatever they're called, these storms have some things in common. They form over ocean water that is at least 80°F (27°C). Heat energy fuels the growth of storm clouds that slowly spin, creating what's called a tropical depression. These spinning storm clouds have low air pressure and the potential to become a bigger storm.

When the storm's winds reach 39 miles an hour (63 km/h), the storm is called a tropical storm and is given a name, taken from lists created by the World Meteorological Organization. A name makes it easier to tell storms apart if several form around the same time in the same ocean.

The storm becomes a full-blown hurricane, cyclone, or typhoon when its winds reach 74 miles an hour (119 km/h). In contrast to the swirling winds on a storm's edges, the storm's center, called the eye, is mostly calm. The sun may even be shining! But watch out for the clouds right around the eye, called the eyewall. They send the storm's strongest winds and heaviest rains.

Did You Know?

A hurricane's winds can create about as much energy as half the world's electrical power plants produce in one year.

BY THE NUMBERS

Hurricane strength is typically labeled as Category 1, 2, 3, 4, or 5, based on the speed of the hurricane's sustained winds. The Saffir-Simpson scale measures a hurricane's strength, with 1 being the weakest and 5 the strongest.

CATEGORY	SUSTAINED WINDS	AMOUNT OF DAMAGE
1	74–95 mph (119–153 km/h)	Very dangerous winds will produce some damage.
2	96–110 mph (154–177 km/h)	Extremely dangerous winds will cause extensive damage.
3 (major)	111–129 mph (178–208 km/h)	Devastating damage will occur.
4 (major)	130–156 mph (209–251 km/h)	Catastrophic damage will occur.
5 (major)	157 mph or higher (252 km/h or higher)	Catastrophic damage will occur.

All Eyes
ON THE STORM

Weather Words

"It's sort of like riding a roller coaster through a car wash."

—hurricane hunter Richard Henning, on what it's like to fly through a storm

DEBRIS FROM HURRICANE KATRINA

Hurricanes can cause havoc if they come ashore. A single storm, like Hurricane Katrina in 2005, can cause billions of dollars in damage to homes, stores, roads, bridges, and other structures—not to mention the terrible loss of life. And the biggest tropical cyclones can be killers, too, because of their high winds and floods caused by their pounding rains.

With so much at stake, it's no surprise that the U.S. government hires a lot of hurricane experts. Their jobs include trying to predict where storms will hit, tracking them as they near the shore, and recording how much damage they cause. Here's a look at two agencies that keep an eye on hurricanes.

ON THE HUNT FOR HURRICANES

When you hear a local weather report, chances are some of the information came from the National Oceanic and Atmospheric Administration (NOAA). This agency is the top source for all things weather.

NOAA's daring hurricane hunters fly in specially equipped planes. When most aircraft are grounded because of wild weather, these planes head for the heart of the hurricane. They fly into the storm's eyewall, where winds can reach more than 150 miles an hour (241 km/h). Scientists onboard measure a storm's wind speed and direction, humidity, and air pressure. That info helps the hunters know if a storm is getting stronger and how much damage it could cause from winds or a storm surge. One hurricane hunter aircraft can also fly high above hurricanes, gathering info about the upper atmosphere near the storm.

CENTERS OF ATTENTION

Keeping an eye on tropical cyclones before they near land is the job of two NOAA agencies. The National Hurricane Center tracks the storms that form in the Atlantic Ocean and the northern Pacific Ocean, while the Central Pacific Hurricane Center has the same job for other parts of the Pacific. The meteorologists at the centers use satellites, radar, and information gathered by planes to watch where storms go after they form. The goal is to warn people who are in a hurricane's path so they can prepare to shelter from the storm—or flee, if staying in their location is too risky.

NOAA also makes predictions at the start of each hurricane season. They try to estimate how many named storms will form and how many might become major hurricanes. But predicting storms is tricky business. In 2020, the center predicted there would be eight hurricanes. In reality, there were 14!

THE NATIONAL HURRICANE CENTER, MIAMI, FLORIDA, U.S.A.

NOAA HURRICANE HUNTERS

HURRICANE SEASON
IN THE UNITED STATES

ATLANTIC OCEAN:
JUNE 1 TO NOVEMBER 30

Peak activity: September

Average number of hurricanes each year: 7

EASTERN PACIFIC OCEAN:
MAY 15 TO NOVEMBER 30

Peak activity: Late June to early October

Average number of hurricanes each year: 8

CENTRAL PACIFIC OCEAN:
JUNE 1 TO NOVEMBER 30

Peak activity: No specific range

Average number of hurricanes each year: 2

HURRICANE WARNING

Wild Facts
ABOUT WEATHER

THE **LARGEST HAILSTONE** ON RECORD IN THE UNITED STATES FELL IN SOUTH DAKOTA IN 2010. IT WAS **EIGHT INCHES** (20 CM) ACROSS AND WEIGHED ALMOST **TWO POUNDS** (0.9 KG).

>>A **MIRAGE** LOOKS LIKE **WATER,** BUT IT'S ACTUALLY JUST A **REFLECTION** OF THE **SKY** THAT **FORMS** ON A LAYER OF **HOT AIR.**

IN CHINA, PEOPLE ONCE FLEW **KITES** TO JUDGE THE **STRENGTH OF THE WIND.**

EACH YEAR, ABOUT **100,000** THUNDERSTORMS FORM ACROSS THE UNITED STATES.

>>AN **AVALANCHE** ON A SNOW-COVERED MOUNTAIN CAN REACH A SPEED OF **80 MILES AN HOUR** (130 KM/H) IN JUST **FIVE SECONDS.**

IT TAKES ABOUT **100,000 DROPLETS** OF WATER IN A CLOUD TO FORM ONE SNOWFLAKE.

Snowballs are WAY more fun than hair balls.

THE WORLD'S LARGEST **SNOWBALL FIGHT** INCLUDED **7,681 PEOPLE** HURLING THE BALLS AT ONCE.

TYPHOON TIP, THE MOST POWERFUL TROPICAL CYCLONE EVER, HAD A **WIDTH OF ALMOST 1,400 MILES** (2,253 KM)—ABOUT THE DISTANCE FROM **NEW YORK CITY TO DALLAS, TEXAS.**

Typhoon Tip width compared to the contiguous U.S.

UNITED STATES

TYPHOON TIP

New York

1,380 miles (2,221 km)

Dallas

ATLANTIC OCEAN

PACIFIC OCEAN

Gulf of Mexico

SEVERE WEATHER WARNING! WHAT TO DO

It pays to be prepared!

3NG NEWS

EVACUATION ROUTE

What can you and your family do to stay safe when a hurricane is heading toward your town? How can you protect yourself when a tornado threatens to touch down near you? Here are some tips.

BE PREPARED!

Thanks to high-tech weather forecasting, people in the path of a hurricane usually have time to prepare before a major storm strikes. A forecast might issue a hurricane watch, which means a storm could hit a certain area. A warning means hurricane-strength winds are expected in that area.

The Centers for Disease Control and Prevention and the Department of Homeland Security recommend you take the following steps if you live in an area where hurricanes are a threat:

- Keep emergency numbers programmed into cell phones, such as 911 or relatives you might need to contact.
- Know how to get to emergency shelters in your area.
- Prepare an emergency supply kit.
- If you have a pet, make plans to go to a shelter or other safe place where you can bring them with you.
- Make sure the family car has a full tank of gas.
- Cover windows with plywood or plastic.
- Keep up-to-date on the forecast.
- Bring inside any outdoor items that could blow around, such as wind chimes, patio furniture, and potted plants.

TORNADO TIPS

You won't have much time to prepare if you hear reports of a tornado near you or you actually see one approaching. But the National Weather Service has some tips for how to stay safe:

- Go to a basement or the lowest level of a building.
- Stay away from windows and doors that lead outside.
- Stay in a closet or other space toward the center of your home, away from outermost walls.
- Try to protect your head.
- If possible, go under a heavy table or other piece of sturdy furniture.
- If you're outside, try to find a ditch, cover your head with your hands, and stay low.
- If you live in an area prone to tornadoes, keep an emergency kit like the one for hurricanes.

EMERGENCY SUPPLY KIT

- ☐ one gallon (3.8 L) of water per person for several days
- ☐ at least several days' worth of food that won't spoil, such as canned foods
- ☐ battery-powered or hand crank radio
- ☐ flashlight (make sure it works!)
- ☐ first aid kit
- ☐ extra batteries
- ☐ manual can opener for food
- ☐ cell phone with chargers and a backup battery
- ☐ essential prescription medicines
- ☐ change of clothes
- ☐ blanket
- ☐ cash

FIRST AID

SURVIVOR STORIES: HURRICANE HEROES

HURRICANE MARIA AFTERMATH, TOA BAJA, PUERTO RICO

Puerto Rico & U.S. Virgin Islands, U.S.A.

The people of Puerto Rico knew a powerful hurricane was on its way. On September 20, 2017, Hurricane Maria was a Category 5 storm when it ripped through the U.S. Virgin Islands, devastating the island of St. Croix with its powerful winds. It then headed to Puerto Rico, about 100 miles (161 km) away. Now a Category 4 storm, it still packed winds of 155 miles an hour

(249 km/h). The storm's rains reached the island even sooner, and in about 48 hours, more than two feet (0.6 m) of rain would fall in some areas.

SEEKING SHELTER

In Toa Baja, a community near Puerto Rico's capital of San Juan, Carmen Chévere Ortiz knew the danger Maria posed. Milly, as her friends called her, had lived through earlier hurricanes that devastated Puerto Rico. As Maria's rains pounded down, Milly watched the water rise from a nearby creek. And then rise some more. Soon, she ordered her children and her mother into the family car to head for safety. As she drove, Milly shouted a warning to her neighbors that the area was flooding.

Milly and the cars that followed her headed to a local school, which was on higher ground. The fence to the school was locked. Milly made a decision—the people fleeing the flood should break the lock and enter the school. It was their best chance to survive.

TAKING CHARGE

Once inside the school, Milly once again took the lead. She found food for the growing number of people seeking safety at the school. At night, she assigned people to different rooms and recorded everyone's name. Milly's group named the school the Ark, a reference to the biblical story of Noah and the ark he built to escape a flood. Milly and several other people used kayaks to rescue people trapped in their homes and brought them to the Ark.

The victims of Maria's flood stayed at the Ark for several days. Many then moved to an official shelter. Milly and her neighbors' homes were badly damaged by the flood, which in spots was 20 feet (6 m) deep. But they had survived.

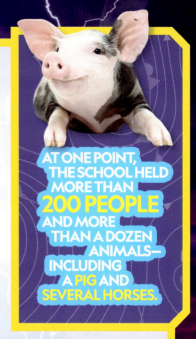

AT ONE POINT, THE SCHOOL HELD MORE THAN **200 PEOPLE** AND MORE THAN A DOZEN ANIMALS— INCLUDING A **PIG** AND SEVERAL HORSES.

DAMAGE TO TOA BAJA, PUERTO RICO, AFTER HURRICANE MARIA

DAMAGING HURRICANES TO HIT PUERTO RICO

NAME	YEAR	CATEGORY
Hugo	1989	3
Georges	1998	3
Irma	2017	5
Maria	2017	4
Fiona	2022	4

HURRICANE MARIA

Deadly DROUGHTS

I need a much bigger watering can.

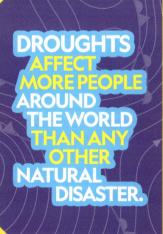

DROUGHTS AFFECT MORE PEOPLE AROUND THE WORLD THAN ANY OTHER NATURAL DISASTER.

Too much rain can be destructive. But what happens when there's not enough? Or any at all? A drought is any extended period of dry weather. What is considered a drought in normally rainy areas, such as along parts of the Pacific Coast in the United States, might be different from a drought in the usually sunny and dry southwestern states. But regardless of the location, droughts can cause crops and farm animals to die, dry conditions that can lead to forest fires, and a significant reduction in the supply of drinking water. Droughts also often force people to make changes in their daily lives. People in drought-ridden communities might have to stop washing their cars, water their gardens and lawns less, and take shorter showers. Governments sometimes pass laws to make sure people follow these water-reduction rules.

A FARM IN WESTERN TEXAS DURING THE DUST BOWL

DEADLY DROUGHTS

Droughts can last for a few months, or they can go on for many years. One of the most famous droughts in the United States happened during the 1930s. Starting in 1931, four periods of drought hit parts of Kansas, Oklahoma, Colorado, Texas, and New Mexico. The lack of rain, some bad farming practices, and strong winds created huge dust storms, which led to the region being called the Dust Bowl. By the end of the decade, around 7,000 people had died, many from lack of food or from dust inhalation. Another two million had to leave their homes to find safer places to live.

In Australia, a drought that started in 1997 lasted until 2009. Nicknamed the Millennium Drought, it hit the southern part of the country hard. The city of Melbourne had below-average rainfall every year. As in the United States, the drought brought dust storms and destroyed crops; more than half of Australia's farmland was hit by the drought. Extreme heat toward the end of the drought killed almost 400 people. Wildfires killed another 173 people and destroyed thousands of homes. Droughts and wildfires such as these also have a huge impact on wild animals.

Did You Know?

Arica, Chile, holds the record for the longest dry spell—more than 14 years without rain!

WAYBACK WEATHER: N-ICE WORK

More than 1,000 years ago, the Puebloan people of what is today New Mexico found a cool way to survive several long dry spells. In this region, volcanic formations called lava tubes are found underground. These long tubes were formed by lava that flowed through the region many years before. Over time, these large underground spaces filled with water and were cold enough for the water to freeze. The Puebloans ventured into these spaces, called "ice caves," and burned small fires to melt the ice.

In the Know
ON SNOW

SNOW SHOW

Here are the four categories of snowflakes:

Plates are one of the common types of flakes. These six-sided particles form when the temperature is just below 32°F (0°C) or below 5°F (–15°C).

Columns don't stick together as well as other kinds of flakes, so they don't make good snowballs.

Needles, as the name suggests, are long and thin. Unlike columns, they pack together nicely.

Dendrites form when there is a lot of moisture in the air, and they make the fluffiest snow. The name means "tree-like," and these flakes have six main "branches" with smaller branches sprouting from them.

Did You Know?

The Inuit people of Greenland have one word for snow in the air—*qanik*—and another for snow on the ground—*aputi*.

Snow can be fun! Maybe you live in a region that gets snow and you're familiar with these white flakes—you can go sledding or skiing, make a snow fort, or cozy up under a blanket as you watch the flakes fall. But too much snow, like in a blizzard (see page 62), can cause a lot of problems. The storms can create hard, blowing snow called a whiteout, which makes it hard to see what's in front of you. This can be especially dangerous while driving.

What is snow exactly? Snow starts as ice crystals that come together in clouds with temperatures close to 0°F (–18°C). It can take just a few crystals to form a snowflake, though some flakes have up to 200 crystals. Scientists have seen more than 100 different kinds of snowflakes. Here's the lowdown on snow.

Cool Facts
ABOUT SNOW

A MAMMOTH SNOWFLAKE FELL IN MONTANA IN 1887—IT WAS **15 INCHES** (38 CM) **WIDE!**

>> SOME U.S. TOWNS HAVE CONTESTS TO NAME THEIR SNOWPLOWS. NAMES INCLUDE BLIZZARD OF OZ, FAST AND FLURRIOUS, AND CLEAROPATHRA.

>> THE FIRST KNOWN DRAWING OF A SNOWMAN IS ALMOST 750 YEARS OLD.

SOME ANIMALS IN COLD REGIONS, SUCH AS ARCTIC FOXES AND POLAR BEARS, HAVE SPECIAL VISION SO THEY CAN SEE DURING WHITEOUTS.

ON AVERAGE, ABOUT **12 INCHES** (30 CM) OF SNOW IS THE SAME AMOUNT OF PRECIPITATION AS **ONE INCH** (2.5 CM) OF RAIN.

SNOW LOOKS WHITE, BUT SNOWFLAKES ARE ACTUALLY CLEAR.

BLIZZARD!

Snowmaggedon! Snowpocalypse! Snowzilla!

3NG NEWS

IN REDFIELD, NEW YORK, LAKE-EFFECT SNOW IN 2007 LASTED FOR 10 DAYS, DROPPING NEARLY ENOUGH SNOW TO COVER A SINGLE-STORY HOUSE.

When a big snowstorm hits, some people love to come up with catchy names to suggest its power. But there's an old-fashioned name for the worst winter storm—a blizzard. Not all massive snow events count as blizzards. A "snowzilla" that hit the Washington, D.C., area in 2016 dropped up to 30 inches (76 cm) of snow over two days, but it wasn't a blizzard. What does make a snowstorm a blizzard?

BLIZZARD SPECIFICS

A blizzard is a specific brew of things. Strong wind is one

ingredient. With big winter storms, the air pressure inside the storm is lower than the pressure on the west side of it. The difference in air pressure creates strong winds. To earn blizzard status, the storm's winds have to reach 35 miles an hour (56 km/h). And those wicked winds can combine with cold temperatures to create a windchill as low as −60°F (−51°C)!

The second ingredient of a blizzard is low visibility, or a reduction in how far you can see. The snow has to fall fast and hard or blow around enough for this to happen. In a blizzard, snow cuts visibility to less than one-quarter mile (0.4 km) for at least three hours.

MORE WINTER WALLOPS

Another big winter storm is called a nor'easter. That's a short form of the word "northeastern," which refers to the direction of the storm's main winds. These storms form along the East Coast of the United States, usually between Georgia and New Jersey. Then they move northward. These storms are fueled by the difference in temperature between cold air that pours in from Canada and warmer air along coastal waters. Nor'easters can form in summer, too, bringing rain instead of snow, but the strongest ones come in winter. Along with lots of snow, they can pack high winds and can cause flooding along the shore.

Cold and warm air help whip up another winter wonder. Some areas along the Great Lakes of the United States and Canada get hit with lake-effect snowstorms. Cold air blows across the lakes and mixes with the warmer air over the water. The air rises and forms storm clouds that can dump a lot of snow in a small area.

WAYBACK WEATHER: A REALLY BIG SNOW

Spring was just around the corner in March 1888, when the worst blizzard in U.S. history hit the East Coast. This powerful storm hung out over several states for three days. Persistent winds reached 60 miles an hour (97 km/h), and some cities got up to 50 inches (127 cm) of snow—snowdrifts in one New York town reached up to 40 feet (12 m)! This "Great Blizzard" was perhaps the deadliest ever, killing more than 400 people. The damage the storm caused led New York City to start putting tracks for city trains underground, creating the subways still used today.

Did You Know?

In 1978, a nor'easter that hit several New England states dropped more than two feet (0.6 m) of snow in some areas and left 10,000 cars stranded on roads.

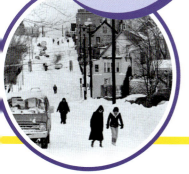

SURVIVOR STORIES:
TRAPPED ON A MOUNTAIN

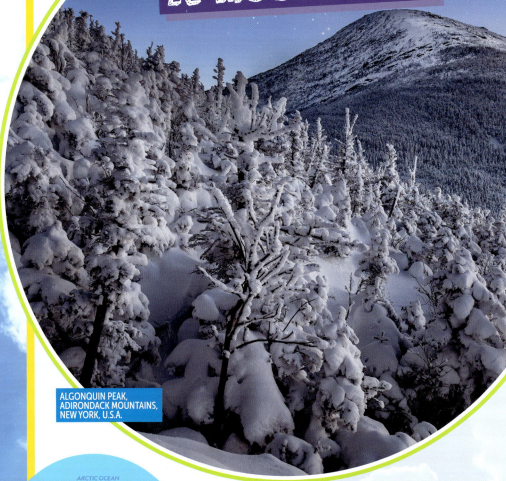

ALGONQUIN PEAK,
ADIRONDACK MOUNTAINS,
NEW YORK, U.S.A.

ARCTIC OCEAN

NORTH
AMERICA
EUROPE
Algonquin Peak,
U.S.A.
ASIA
AFRICA
PACIFIC
OCEAN
PACIFIC
OCEAN
SOUTH
AMERICA
INDIAN
OCEAN
AUSTRALIA
ATLANTIC
OCEAN
SOUTHERN OCEAN
ANTARCTICA

On December 11, 2016, Blake Alois, 20, and Maddie Popolizio, 19, headed for a mountain called Algonquin Peak. At just over 5,000 feet (1,524 m), it's the second highest summit in New York's Adirondack Mountains. The pair were prepared for an exciting adventure. They brought snowshoes to help them climb snowy trails, and their backpacks were stuffed with food and water. But Blake and Maddie didn't know what waited for them on the mountain.

STUMBLE AND TUMBLE

Blake and Maddie reached the top of Algonquin around noon. What had started as a sunny day was turning murky, as a thick fog began to surround them. Soon, heading back down the mountain, they could barely see a few feet in front of them. They lost sight of the trail and didn't know which way to go. Snow started falling and the wind began to howl.

Maddie and Blake headed in what they hoped was the right direction. But with the blowing snow, it was almost impossible to see, and the pair stumbled off the trail. They fell a hundred feet (30 m) through snow that was at least three feet (0.9 m) deep. Some of it got into Maddie's jacket, gloves, and boots. She couldn't feel her legs and feet. Blake emptied his backpack of food and used it to try to warm her.

The pair had landed on top of some snow-covered trees. They were able to flatten out some of the snow and set up a place to sit. Their cellphones were useless in the remote spot, so they yelled for help. No one was around to hear their cries.

RESCUED AT LAST

Through the night, Blake and Maddie huddled together to try to stay warm. They ate what was left of their food, including cookies and granola bars. They held their water bottles close to their bodies to melt the frozen liquid inside. The next day, though, the lack of water and the freezing conditions began to affect Maddie. She thought she heard voices of people nearby, when really no one was there.

Finally, on the morning of December 13, Maddie heard something that was real—the sound of a rescue helicopter. The two began to call out, and then the voice of forest ranger Scott Van Laer responded. He and a volunteer searcher soon reached Blake and Maddie and gave them food and hot tea and warmed them with clothes and a blanket.

Bad weather prevented the helicopter from lifting the pair out for two hours. They both suffered from frostbite and a condition called hypothermia, which results from being in the cold for too long. In extreme conditions, hypothermia can be deadly. But Blake and Maddie were going to be okay. They had survived their wintry disaster.

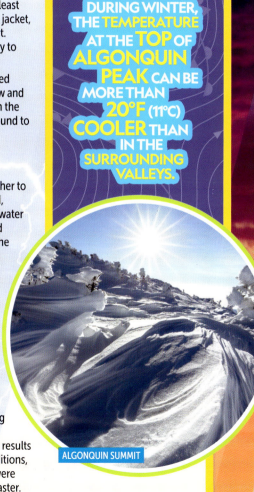

DURING WINTER, THE TEMPERATURE AT THE TOP OF ALGONQUIN PEAK CAN BE MORE THAN 20°F (11°C) COOLER THAN IN THE SURROUNDING VALLEYS.

ALGONQUIN SUMMIT

Icy, YOU SEE

Watch out! It's slick out here! Icy roads can send cars spinning wildly, and an icy sidewalk can slip you up. Ice can fall from storm clouds or form as temperatures drop and water freezes. And you might be surprised to discover that some of the biggest, baddest frozen stuff doesn't come in winter at all! Here's a look at icy weather in its different forms.

SLEET

Sleet starts off as snow, but as it falls and hits a patch of warm air, it melts a bit, then refreezes when it reaches colder air near the ground. It lands as frozen drops up to the size of a pea that can accumulate just like snow—but harder and icier!

ICE JAMS

When temperatures stay below freezing for a long time, ice forms on rivers and lakes. Then, when it warms up a bit, the ice breaks into chunks that can create ice jams as they build up near obstacles in the water. The jams can block a flowing river, causing a flood.

FREEZING RAIN

This icy stuff forms after snowflakes melt as they move through warm air. The newly formed raindrops are still cold as they reach the ground, and when the temperature is cold enough, the drops freeze on hard surfaces, sometimes forming a layer of ice. When at least ¼ inch (0.6 cm) of freezing rain accumulates on surfaces, it's officially an ice storm.

FROST

If you live in an area that gets colder temperatures, you may have gone outside one morning and seen glistening frost on low-lying plants like grass, or maybe on a window. This thin layer of ice forms as water vapor cools down, turning it into a liquid. Then, the water freezes from cold air. Frost usually forms at night and often in valleys. Cold air is heavier than warm air, so it sinks toward the ground.

HAIL

If it's hailing, best to get indoors! This frozen precipitation can be big enough to damage crops and dent cars, and you certainly wouldn't want to be hit with a piece. Hail forms in thunderstorms, high in the coldest parts of the clouds. Ice droplets fall in the clouds and then updrafts bring them back up, where they collide with water droplets, which then freeze, making the hailstone bigger. This repetitive down and up movement can go on for a while, making even bigger hailstones that finally fall to Earth.

BLACK ICE

This ice isn't really black; it just looks that way when it forms on a dark road. It often appears when snow or ice on a road melts during the day, then freezes when temperatures cool down at night. It can be especially hard to see on roads.

WAYBACK WEATHER: NOT NICE ICE

North America's worst ice storm in years hit northern New England and New York in the United States, and parts of southern Canada in January 1998. Over several days, freezing rain created ice on surfaces that in some spots was up to four inches (10 cm) thick. Ice-covered branches snapped off and fell onto homes, cars, and power lines. Millions of people lost electricity. For some of them, the lights were out for several weeks. In Canada, 35 people died in the Great Ice Storm of 1998, making it one of that country's worst natural disasters. The storm killed about 40 people in the U.S.

Icy SECRETS

FROZEN AIR BUBBLES ON LAKE BAIKAL, SIBERIA, RUSSIA

GLACIERS HOLD ALMOST 75 PERCENT OF EARTH'S FRESH WATER.

Did you know that some ice found in Antarctica is almost four million years old? That makes Earth's glaciers seem like babies in comparison! By contrast, the oldest glacier in Alaska is about 30,000 years old (which is still really old!). And across Earth, scientists are studying this ancient ice to discover what secrets it might hold.

For example, air bubbles trapped in the ice can tell scientists what Earth's atmosphere was like when the ice formed. That gives them important information about our planet's history, even the age before humans existed. Some scientists study ice because they want to know how levels of the gas carbon dioxide have changed over time. Carbon dioxide is one of the gases that is causing global warming (see page 144). Looking into Earth's icy past could help us understand how much the planet's temperatures might rise in the future.

Did You Know?

With its thick ice layers, Antarctica has the highest average elevation of all continents.

Welcome to my lib*rrrr*ary.

A GOOD CRY(OSPHERE)

All the frozen material on Earth is called its cryosphere ("cryo" comes from a Greek word meaning "icy cold"). It includes ice and snow on land, most of which is in ice sheets in Greenland and Antarctica. Other ice and snow on land make up glaciers, ice caps, and permafrost—sand, gravel, and bits of organic matter glued together by bits of ice. In water, the cryosphere includes frozen rivers and lakes and icebergs. Ice shelves form when ice on land merges with the sea.

The cryosphere plays an important role in shaping Earth's climate. It reflects some of the sun's energy back into space, which helps regulate temperatures on the ground. And ice on land stores water. When glaciers melt, they can provide water for people and crops nearby. But across the planet, too much melting ice poses some problems. Global warming is melting more of the cryosphere, leading to rising sea levels and higher temperatures where the ice cover is lost (see page 150).

WHERE IN THE WORLD?
A VERY COOL COLLECTION

A special "library" of sorts in Copenhagen, Denmark, offers a chilling checkout! The Centre for Ice and Climate at the Niels Bohr Institute holds a huge collection of ice taken from ice cores. These are long, tube-shaped pieces of ice retrieved from all over planet Earth. Some of the ice is tens of thousands of years old and came from depths of 7,874 feet (2,400 m). Scientists from all over the world take small samples of the cores for their research. But unlike with library books, they don't have to return the ice—it melts!

Measuring UP

BAROMETER

A barometer measures air pressure. Falling air pressure means a storm is on the way, while rising pressures signal a return to sunny skies.

Meteorology is a science that studies changes in Earth's atmosphere that create our weather. Meteorologists measure what's happening at any given moment using all sorts of tools. Some are high tech, as you'll see on page 72. Some are a bit simpler, and you might even have them at home! Here are some tools of the trade.

ANEMOMETER

Take this tool out for a spin when you want to know how fast the wind is blowing.

DEW POINT HYGROMETER

This device measures the amount of moisture in the air. A high dew point equals high humidity—which can make you feel hot and sticky!

THERMOMETER

This tool tells you exactly how hot it is. For many years, thermometers used a liquid metal called mercury, which rose or fell inside a tube as the temperature changed. Today, digital thermometers are more common.

WEATHER VANE

The letters on this gadget indicate the four cardinal directions—north, south, east, and west—and it's topped with a pointer that shows which way the wind is blowing.

RAIN GAUGE

When the rain, rain, won't go away, this device can tell you exactly how much fell.

MAPPING THE WEATHER

Meteorologists use special symbols on a map to explain what's happening with the weather. Here are a few of them.

ATLANTIC OCEAN

UNITED STATES

PACIFIC OCEAN

Gulf of Mexico

MAP KEY

H — High pressure center

L — Low pressure center

— Warm front

— Cold front

— Stationary front

Capital H's and L's indicate areas of high and low pressure. In the Northern Hemisphere, winds move clockwise around a high area and counterclockwise around a low one. In the Southern Hemisphere, those directions are reversed.

Warm fronts show where warm air is moving in to replace colder air. The little half circles show the direction of the cold air that will be pushed out.

Stationary fronts are boundaries between cold and warm air masses that move slowly or don't move at all. They can bring cloudy weather and long spells of precipitation in one area.

Fronts are boundaries between air masses with different temperatures, wind speed, and moisture. Cold fronts push out warmer masses of air. They can create strong winds and bring colder temperatures and precipitation. The triangles on the line point in the direction that the front is moving.

WEATHER HERO: GREAT GREEK

In ancient Greece, *meteoron* referred to anything that was in the sky. Around 350 B.C.E., a Greek philosopher and scientist named Aristotle wrote about things in the sky in his book *Meteorologica*. He wasn't always right—he thought Earth, not the sun, was at the center of our solar system. And he didn't know that Earth rotates, which affects the weather. But he did describe such things as clouds, wind, rain, and snow. For example, Aristotle correctly believed that the sun's heat turns water on the ground into a vapor that rises into the air and then turns into precipitation. His ideas shaped how others thought about the weather for 2,000 years.

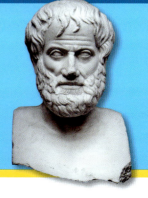

Sky-High EYES

Some weather tools fit in your hands. But some are too big—and too far away—for that. The International Space Station (ISS) is just one of the "eyes in the sky" that help meteorologists predict the weather. Here's the scoop on the ISS, as well as some other big devices that help us detect weather.

THE ISS

Circling some 230 miles (370 km) above Earth, the ISS gives a bird's-eye view of tropical cyclones. In 2022, the United States began testing two sensors on the station designed to collect specific weather data. One measures wind speed and direction right above oceans, and the other measures how much water is in the atmosphere. That information can help forecasters make better predictions about where storms will form and how strong they'll be.

RADAR

Radar helps us "see" using radio waves. The waves bounce off precipitation and other things in the atmosphere, then return to their source. A computer analyzes how strong the returning signal is and how fast it traveled. A special kind of radar, called Doppler, can detect the movement of air within a storm, along with the location and strength of its precipitation.

DOPPLER RADAR CAN SEND OUT AND RECEIVE ABOUT 1,300 RADIO WAVES IN ONE SECOND.

SAILDRONES

Ahoy, matey! Not all drones soar overhead. Some sail the seas in search of weather data. The National Oceanic and Atmospheric Administration (NOAA) uses saildrones to track hurricanes. Along with collecting data about temperature, air pressure, and wind speed, these drones can also measure wave height. The seaworthy saildrones are powered by the sun, wind, and energy from the waves.

WEATHER BALLOONS

Some weather tools go up, up, and away an old-fashioned way: They hitch a ride on weather balloons. A gas lighter than air helps the balloon rise about 22 miles (35 km) into the atmosphere. A sensor called a radiosonde collects info on the temperature and humidity, and radios the data back to Earth.

STAY WEATHER-ALERT

After meteorologists study the data collected by all their tools, they need to let people know what's ahead. In the United States, NOAA has several ways to alert people about approaching weather dangers. Its Weather Radio All Hazards broadcasts weather watches and warnings, using information from local National Weather Service (NWS) offices. More than a thousand radio transmitters send out the alerts across all 50 states and to U.S. territories. NWS can also send out alerts by text message. This is part of a larger system, called Wireless Emergency Alerts, used during emergencies by other government agencies.

DRONES

Along with hurricane hunter aircraft (see page 50), drones can track tropical cyclones to record the storms' temperature, pressure, and humidity. In 2022, NOAA sent a drone into the eye of a storm for the first time, which is much safer than having a person fly a plane into certain parts of the eye.

Severe alert

National Weather Service: SEVERE THUNDERSTORM WARNING in effect for this area until 6:30 PM CST for DESTRUCTIVE 80 mph winds. Take shelter in a sturdy building, away from windows. Flying debris may be deadly to those caught without shelter.

OK

A little hot there, big guy?

98°

DANIEL FAHRENHEIT

Your body is a kind of thermometer. When it gets really cold, your teeth might chatter. A hot, humid day can make you sweat. But to know exactly how hot or cold it is, you turn to a thermometer. Here's a little fun history on how we got the handy tool that measures the weather.

"FAHR" ENOUGH

Thermometers are scales, but instead of measuring weight, they show the temperature at any given moment. Daniel Fahrenheit, the inventor of the scale with his name, introduced the first practical, precise thermometer in 1714. He used the liquid metal mercury to measure the temperature. Fahrenheit used 0° as the base temperature when a mixture of water and salt froze. On his original scale, 30° was the temperature when water without salt froze, and 240° was the boiling point of water. Fahrenheit later updated his scale, using 32° as the freezing point of water and a lower boiling point of 205° (212° is the boiling point for his scale today). Fahrenheit's scale is used in the United States and only a handful of other countries, including Belize, the Bahamas, and Saint Kitts and Nevis.

"C" HERE

About 30 years after Fahrenheit started his work, another scientist came up with a different scale. Anders Celsius suggested the boiling point of water should be 0° and the freezing point 100°. Then, another scientist suggested the boiling point should be the higher number, so it was set at 100° and the freezing point was made 0°. That stuck, giving us the Celsius scale that is used today. (Both Celsius and Fahrenheit scales also use negative numbers, for those really cold days.) Celsius called his scale centigrade. "Centi" comes from the French word for 100, and "grade" from the Latin word meaning "step." Celsius's scale had 100 steps, or degrees, between the freezing and boiling points.

Did You Know?

To honor Anders Celsius, the centigrade scale was renamed for him in 1948.

ANDERS CELSIUS

GOING TO EXTREMES

BY THE NUMBERS

Need to convert from Fahrenheit to Celsius or the other way? Here are two formulas that can do the trick.

From F to C:
Subtract 32 and multiply by .5556
Example: (80°F - 32) x .5556 = 26.7°C

From C to F:
Multiply by 1.8 and add 32
Example: (20°C x 1.8) + 32 = 68°F

William Thomson knew something about thermometers, too. Also known as Lord Kelvin, because he was a British lord, Thomson thought scientists needed a new temperature scale to measure the extremes found in the universe. He called his zero "absolute zero"—the temperature at which the tiny particles of matter in something stop moving. That temperature is equal to −459.67°F (−273.15°C). In the Kelvin scale, the temperature markings are called units, not degrees. Outside of science, Kelvin is also used to indicate the color temperature of lightbulbs. A bulb rated 5000K is similar to daylight. One at 2500K is considered warm and ideal for living rooms and bedrooms.

MERCURY EXPANDS AND CONTRACTS WITH CHANGES IN TEMPERATURE. IT IS RARELY USED IN THERMOMETERS TODAY, THOUGH, AS IT CAN BE TOXIC.

WILLIAM THOMSON

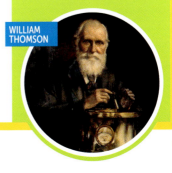

Forecasting FOLKLORE

O ver the years, people have suggested ways to predict the weather that make scientists scoff. Some of these methods have a ring of truth to them, but other beliefs about the weather are definitely not true. Take this quiz to see what you know about some weather myths and mistakes.

Hurricanes and tornadoes are the deadliest forms of extreme weather.

FALSE!

They are powerful storms, but it's much more dangerous to be exposed to extreme temperatures, hot or cold.

"A year of snow, crops will grow"—snowy winters bring good growing seasons.

TRUE!

Layers of snow are filled with air, which acts as a blanket to protect plants from extreme cold. Then, melting snow provides water in the spring.

Lightning never strikes the same spot twice.

FALSE!

Tall and pointed objects, like some buildings, can get hit over and over. And even some people have been struck twice. Over many years, Roy Sullivan of Virginia was struck by lightning seven times. Casey Wagner of Texas was jolted by bolts twice on the same day!

And speaking of lightning—if you touch someone who's been struck by a bolt, you can receive a bad electrical shock.

FALSE!

A body can't store electricity, so someone hit by lightning can't electrocute someone by touching them.

The old saying, "Red sky at night, sailor's delight" means the next day should be pleasant.

TRUE!

When the sun sets and the sky is particularly clear, more red and orange light strikes our eyes. And a clear sky at night often means the next day will at least start off without any storms.

You'll catch a cold if you go outside in winter with wet hair.

FALSE!

You catch a cold after you've been exposed to a virus, not because of your wet hair. But there are some conditions that make it easier to catch a cold during winter. For one, viruses like colder temperatures, and they can thrive in your nose, which can get cold when you're outside. And because we often spend more time indoors during cold weather and we're around other people, we might catch colds from them.

A ring around the moon can mean wet weather is on its way.

TRUE!

Meteorologists call that ring a halo, and one can form when moonlight bounces off ice crystals that form in high clouds. The amount of water vapor in the clouds increases before precipitation arrives, so the halo could be a fair forecaster.

Nature's FORECASTERS?

Here, fishy fishy ...

an a cricket tell you the temperature? Do spiders know when cold weather is coming? Many of the folktales about how to predict the weather involve animals of all sorts—and some of these tales are at least partly true! Animals may not be able to give a forecast like a meteorologist, but they can sense changes in the atmosphere that humans can't detect.

UNDER PRESSURE

Some animals are sensitive to changes in air pressure. When the pressure drops, it means stormy weather is on the way. Some sparrows and other birds can feel that drop, so they know it's time to seek shelter from the storm. Some fish might detect changes in water pressure that also signal a storm is coming.

An approaching storm also makes a noise too low in frequency for humans to hear. (Low-pitched sounds, like a bass drum, create sound waves of low frequency, while a flute's high-pitched sounds create higher-frequency waves.) But some animals can hear these low frequencies, or infrasounds. A storm's low sounds can act like an alarm, alerting the animals to find cover.

WARBLER WEATHER WONDER

Scientists have observed birds seeming to sense an approaching storm. In 2014, for example, scientists in Tennessee, U.S.A., studying golden-winged warblers saw something unusual. Without warning, the flock flew off—all the way to Florida! A few days later, a powerful thunderstorm hit the area in Tennessee where the birds had been. The storm unleashed dozens of tornadoes. After the storm passed, the birds came back to Tennessee. One of the scientists who tracked the warblers thought the storm's infrasounds had led the birds to seek safety.

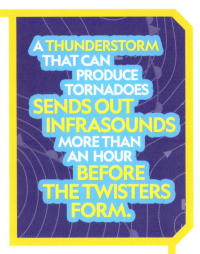

A THUNDERSTORM THAT CAN PRODUCE TORNADOES SENDS OUT INFRASOUNDS MORE THAN AN HOUR BEFORE THE TWISTERS FORM.

Listen up!

THAT'S THE CRICKET

It's no fable or folklore—crickets can sometimes tell you the temperature. The warmer it gets, the faster they rub their wings together. And that rubbing is what makes the chirping sounds crickets are famous for. To use your cricket thermometer, count how many chirps you hear in 15 seconds. Then, add 40 to that number, and you can estimate the temperature in Fahrenheit. This natural thermometer is not foolproof, however, because crickets don't chirp below certain temperatures, plus their age and how hungry they are can also affect the speed of their chirp.

A GOLDEN-WINGED WARBLER

Terrible TEMPERATURES

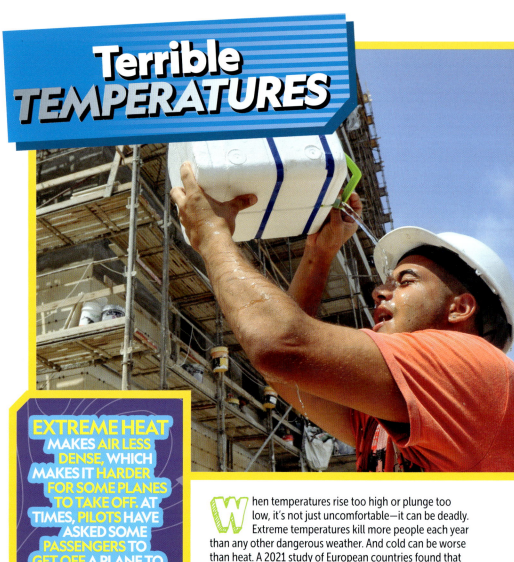

May I have your attention ...

When temperatures rise too high or plunge too low, it's not just uncomfortable—it can be deadly. Extreme temperatures kill more people each year than any other dangerous weather. And cold can be worse than heat. A 2021 study of European countries found that cold spells killed about nine times as many people as heat waves did. But as the climate warms around the world, an increasing number of people are dying from extreme heat. Meteorologists have special terms for some of the conditions that create searing heat and bone-chilling cold.

HEATING UP

In the warmer months, an area of high pressure and warm air called a heat dome can park itself in one spot for days. A heat dome that sat over parts of Europe during the summer of 2023 brought record high temperatures in Italy, Spain, and elsewhere. The central and southern United States also experienced a major heat dome, setting records there, too. All in all, that month was the world's hottest ever recorded.

Sometimes, the temperature doesn't tell the whole heat story. The heat index tells us how temperature and humidity, or moisture in the air, combine to affect the body. During that hot summer of 2023, one spot in the Middle Eastern country of Iran had a heat index of 152°F (67°C).

THE BIG CHILL

All year long, a mass of low pressure with cold air sits over the North and South Poles. This air mass is called a polar vortex, and sometimes during winter in the Northern Hemisphere, part of it swoops down from the North Pole. The roaming polar vortex can bring record cold temperatures and reach areas that usually don't get very cold.

Another blast of extremely cold air is the Siberian Express. It starts in the Arctic regions of Siberia, part of Russia. Then, it barrels eastward, hitting the United States and Canada. It can reach as far south as Florida, forcing people there to search for warmer clothes they rarely need to wear.

As with heat, things can feel colder than the actual temperature, thanks to windchill. That's a combination of temperature and wind speed. Stronger winds mean the air feels colder to your body.

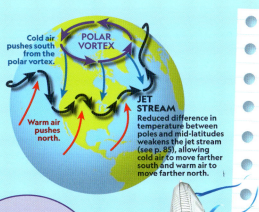

Cold air pushes south from the polar vortex.

POLAR VORTEX

Warm air pushes north.

JET STREAM
Reduced difference in temperature between poles and mid-latitudes weakens the jet stream (see p. 85), allowing cold air to move farther south and warm air to move farther north.

Did You Know?

During a polar vortex in 2023, the windchill at the top of Mount Washington in New Hampshire, U.S.A., reached −108°F (−78°C).

BEAT THE HEAT

You already read about what to do when extreme cold leads to frostbite (page 65). But how can you keep your cool when the heat is on? Staying in hot weather too long can create all kinds of health problems. You can reduce your chance of heat exhaustion or a heat stroke by

☐ staying in air-conditioned spaces as much as possible,

☐ drinking plenty of water,

☐ exercising during the coolest times of the day,

☐ wearing sunscreen while outdoors, and

☐ eating cool foods.

Dire FIRES

A SPECIAL HELICOPTER USED TO FIGHT FIRES DROPS WATER ON A FOREST FIRE.

 ry weather and whipping winds can combine to create a terrible natural disaster: wildfires. These conditions play a big part in fanning the flames.

DRY AND HOT

In the United States, wildfires have their own season—the worst often occur during the summer months. But as the planet warms, wildfires can start any time of year. All a fire needs is plenty of fuel, like dried grass and other plants. Periods of drought can create a lot of this dried material. The fire can start from a lightning strike or other source of heat, such as a dropped match, a spark from an engine, or a downed electrical wire.

Fighting a large wildfire is particularly tricky when humidity is low and the temperature is high. The lack of moisture keeps the fuel dry. High winds are a challenge, too, as they can push the fire into new territory. Some of this occurs with spotting, in which tiny hot embers or sparks are blown by the wind onto fresh fuel. Because of spotting and hot, dry weather conditions, a single wildfire can burn for months.

DEADLY DANGERS

Some of the destruction wildfires cause is obvious. They can burn thousands of acres of trees and kill the wildlife that lives there. As they near towns, wildfires can knock out power lines, destroy homes and other buildings, and kill both livestock and people.

At times, the smoke from wildfires can be almost as bad as the flames. As they burn, the fires release harmful gases into the air. Some of these are the same gases that are increasing global warming. Tiny particles in the smoke can also cause problems for people with breathing issues, such as asthma. Studies done after wildfires in California, U.S.A., showed that children who breathe in smoke are more likely to catch colds and have other health problems.

FIRE DANGER
RED FLAG WARNING
TODAY!
PREVENT FOREST FIRES

GETTING RED-DY

The National Weather Service lets people know when the risk of fires is on the rise by issuing a red flag warning. The warning means three conditions have been detected: Grass and other vegetation on the ground are dry; the humidity will remain low for several hours; and winds 20 feet (6 m) off the ground will blow at 15 miles an hour (24 km/h) or more for several hours. The warning lets people know that fires can spread quickly and that they need to be extra careful to avoid causing a spark. The warning also alerts firefighters to be ready to act.

THE LARGEST WILDFIRE IN U.S. HISTORY BLAZED IN MAINE IN 1825, BURNING AN AREA MORE THAN TWICE THE SIZE OF THE STATE OF DELAWARE.

WILD WINDS

Hold on to your hats!

3NG NEWS

"KATABATIC" COMES FROM A GREEK WORD THAT MEANS "DESCENDING."

Extreme wind events can stoke a forest fire or blow down a building. These events happen all over the world. One major class of winds is called katabatic. Also called fall winds, they usually pop up as gravity pulls cold, dense air down a hillside into warmer air, often around sunset. These winds can lower the humidity or even blow away snow as they move downhill. Let's look at where some of these winds are found.

Santa Ana Winds: These start as cold air that forms over desert mountains east of the Pacific Coast in California, U.S.A. The winds then blow west toward the coast, picking up speed and heat along the way. The warmed winds reach areas that often haven't had rain in months. Because of this, the Santa Anas can fuel massive wildfires.

Williwaw: These katabatic winds are mostly found in two spots that are not anywhere near each other—the Aleutian Islands of Alaska, U.S.A., and South America's Cape of Good Hope. They arise suddenly and blow down cold mountains toward the sea. A williwaw that struck Alaska in 2020 produced wind gusts of 120 miles an hour (193 km/h).

Bora: These katabatic winds get launched when cold air rolls down a region in Europe called the Karst Plateau, toward the Adriatic Sea. Some gusts can reach more than 100 miles an hour (160 km/h). In some areas, people put rocks on their roofs so the bora won't blow away the tiles.

Foehn: Unlike some other katabatic winds, a foehn starts with warm air. It can blow for just a few hours or for several days. These winds form around the world, but they are usually associated with the Alps in Europe. In Switzerland, some people say that when these winds blow, they can cause headaches or depression.

Sirocco: These winds are not katabatic, but they can still pack a punch. Fueled by hot air from the Sahara, they form ahead of storms that head eastward across the Mediterranean Sea. Siroccos affect the countries that border that body of water, such as Spain and Portugal in Europe and Morocco and Tunisia in North Africa. These winds are hot and humid when they reach Europe. In North Africa, they can create dust storms.

Chinook: Named after a Native American tribe that lives in the Pacific Northwest of the United States. With a Chinook, warm air comes in from the Pacific Ocean, cools as it passes over nearby mountains, then warms even more as it moves down the other side of the mountains. Chinooks can rapidly send temperatures soaring by 50°F (28°C).

THE JET SET

To experience really fast winds, you'd have to travel about 30,000 feet (9,100 m) into the atmosphere. That's where narrow bands of winds called jet streams speed along at 275 miles an hour (443 km/h) or more. They form along the boundary where large masses of cold and warm air meet. Within the streams, winds blow from west to east. There are two major kinds of jet streams. The polar ones form close to the North and South Poles. The subtropical ones are located above and below the Equator. Storms are often pushed along by these powerful streams of wind.

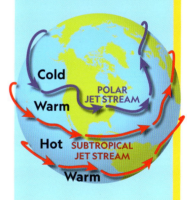

Cold
Warm
POLAR JET STREAM
Hot **SUBTROPICAL JET STREAM**
Warm

SURVIVOR STORIES:
DEADLY WINDS

A HOUSE ON FIRE IN CALIFORNIA

A FIREFIGHTER EXTINGUISHES FLAMES IN CALIFORNIA.

Weather Words

"You can't prepare (mentally) for losing your home. It was hard to believe we lost it ... It was there one day and the next day gone."

—Barbara Warden

The Santa Ana winds were howling October 21, 2007, outside San Diego, California. The winds helped start what's known today as the Witch Creek Fire, one of the worst to hit that part of the state. In a community called Rancho Bernardo, hundreds of homes burned, and several hundred thousand people had to flee their homes. Barbara and Dick Warden were two of them.

BARBARA AND DICK WARDEN

PREPARED, BUT NOT

The Wardens had lived in the area for almost 40 years, so they knew the risk that wildfires posed. As they saw flames approaching during the 2007 fire, they first thought they wouldn't have to evacuate. But the fire spread quickly, as spotting—which is when wind carries pieces of burning material to new locations—carried embers far from the main blaze.

The Wardens didn't wait to be told to leave their home. As the fire closed in, they grabbed just a few things. But they didn't expect to be out of the house long. Barbara only took enough of her work clothes for one day.

When the fire was out, the Wardens returned to find their home destroyed. They soon built a new home in a different part of Rancho Bernardo. And Dick Warden wrote a book describing the family's experience, to try to help others prepare for a wildfire and what might come after.

LEARNING FROM EXPERIENCE

Some of Dick Warden's advice to people who live in areas where wildfires strike is to prepare for the worst before the flames fly. He suggests eight P's—his list of things to take and things to do if forced to evacuate.

Take: People, Pets, Photos, Papers, Personal computer, Possessions of importance

Do: Protect the house by closing doors and windows, and moving outdoor furniture and flammable materials away from the house. Plan ahead by choosing a place where everyone in the household should meet.

Local firefighters also learned from the Witch Creek blaze. Fire companies from different communities now train together so they'll be ready to act as a team if a wildfire hits. These firefighters and others in California can also now watch a system of video cameras that can help spot fires as they start.

WILDFIRE SAFETY

Here are some things you and your family can do to prepare for a possible wildfire.

- [ ] Have a garden hose that can reach every part of your house, to wet it down if necessary.
- [ ] Trim branches that are close to the house.
- [ ] Sweep up dead leaves or branches on the ground.
- [ ] Install and test smoke alarms.
- [ ] If necessary, follow any orders to evacuate.

Otherworldly
WEATHER

Would you believe there is no weather in space? It's true, because space doesn't have an atmosphere. But like Earth, the other planets in our solar system do have weather. So do many of the moons that circle the planets. Here's a look at some of the weather way beyond Earth.

MOON

Close to our home, Earth's moon also lacks an atmosphere. But it does have pockets of ice, in craters near its poles. The ice probably came from comets that hit the moon millions of years ago. It doesn't melt because the sun's heat doesn't reach the craters and the temperature can drop to −400°F (−240°C).

MERCURY

The planet closest to the sun, Mercury has wild swings in temperature—more than 1000°F (555°C) between the sweltering highs and teeth-rattling lows.

VENUS

You wouldn't want to keep your head in the clouds on Venus—the ones surrounding this planet contain sulfuric acid. That oily liquid can eat through metal—and your skin! The planet is also the hottest in our solar system, with average temperatures near 900°F (480°C).

MARS

Winds on the red planet can create clouds of crimson dust. Also striking are dramatic changes in temperature that occur over small differences in height. Because Mars has a very thin atmosphere, heat that the ground absorbs shoots quickly skyward. Standing on Mars's equator at noon, your feet would feel a comfy temperature of 75°F (24°C). But at your head, it would be a chilly 32°F (0°C).

SATURN

Winds near this planet's surface can reach speeds of 500 miles an hour (805 km/h), and they can be twice as fast higher in Saturn's atmosphere. Unlike on Earth, most of the planet's heat comes from deep inside it, not from the sun. The temperature inside Saturn may reach 21,000°F (11,650°C)—about twice as hot as Earth's center.

URANUS

Far from the sun, Uranus sometimes sees the lowest temperatures in the solar system. It drops to −371°F (−224°C) in certain areas. Methane gas in the planet's atmosphere makes it look blue.

JUPITER

Peer through a telescope at Jupiter, and you'll see colorful bands circling the planet. These striking stripes are actually clouds. Along with these clouds come fierce storms, with one that has blown for hundreds of years (see page 48).

NEPTUNE

When it comes to windy, the last planet in the solar system has Saturn beat. Winds on Neptune can hit more than 1,200 miles an hour (2,000 km/h)—more than twice as fast as Saturn's top surface winds. Neptune, along with Uranus, also may have a special kind of "rain" inside the planet. Heat and gases combine to form tiny diamonds. They sink into the even hotter core, where they vaporize and move back up to the cooler levels, where they form solid diamonds again. The pattern keeps repeating—sort of like the water cycle on Earth.

SOLAR STORMS

Another hot topic after the break ...

3NG NEWS

A CORONAL MASS EJECTION CAN TRAVEL AT SPEEDS OF UP TO 6.7 MILLION MILES AN HOUR (10.8 MILLION KM/H)!

Outer space may not have the kind of weather you know, with rain and fog and snow, but the sun does create what scientists call "space weather." The storms in space don't bring strong winds and precipitation to Earth, but they can stir up problems on our planet.

SOLAR STORMS

Just as the sun powers weather on Earth, it also powers weather in space. The sun releases a steady stream of tiny charged particles of plasma. That's a substance formed when a gas is superheated. The plasma creates what's called solar wind. This wind travels far from the sun, speeding at more than one million miles an hour (1.6 million km/h)!

At times, the sun also has strong bursts of electromagnetic energy. These bursts are called solar flares, and they create solar storms. Even bigger than a solar flare is a coronal mass ejection (CME). One of these eruptions can release billions of tons of plasma and lots of magnetic energy.

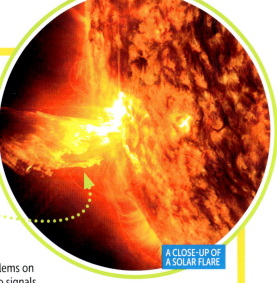

A CLOSE-UP OF A SOLAR FLARE

NO FUN IN THE SUN

Large solar storms and CMEs can cause problems on Earth. The energy they carry can disrupt radio signals sent to and from satellites or that help people communicate on the ground. Solar storms can also cause electrical grids to crash. One powerful storm in 1989 knocked out power across Quebec, Canada, for nine hours.

Just as people want to know if a hurricane or blizzard is heading their way, we Earthlings need to know when a solar storm or CME might zap a satellite or fry a power grid. In the United States, it's the job of NOAA's Space Weather Prediction Center to monitor these events. Using NASA satellites in space and sensors and computers on the ground, the center watches for the development of solar storms. And just as with hurricanes, the space weather forecasters rate the storms on a scale of 1 to 5.

A NOAA SPACE WEATHER FORECASTER

BRIGHT NIGHT LIGHTS

Some solar storms put on a show—a light show, that is. They create auroras—wavy wisps of color that are usually green or yellow, or sometimes red. The auroras appear close to the North and South Poles and are often called the northern and southern lights. Particles of energy called electrons are carried by the solar wind into Earth's atmosphere. The planet is surrounded by a magnetic field, which directs the electrons toward the poles. There, the particles collide with gas molecules in the air, creating a colorful display. In the Northern Hemisphere, the most intense solar storms can create auroras that can be seen as far south as Hawaii, U.S.A.

The Big PICTURE

A 140-YEAR-OLD ALLIGATOR FOSSIL

Let's come back down to Earth. The weather here is linked to climate, but the two are very different. Think of it this way: Weather is like a snapshot of what's happening in the atmosphere at any given moment. Is precipitation falling? What's the temperature, wind speed, and humidity? For weather information to be meaningful, we need to know the time and location that data was measured and observed.

Climate is more like a video—a really long video, with a huge lens that can record what's going on in a large area. To understand a region's climate, meteorologists look at a "video" that's at least 30 years long.

CLIMATE CLUES

Climate in one region can change over time. And the natural world has recorded some of these changes. You read about the library filled with ancient ice (see page 69). Another way to study past climate is by looking at the rings inside trees. Some trees add a new ring every

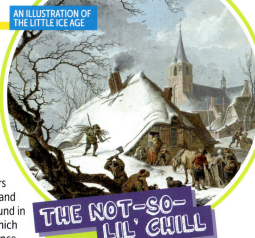

year. During wet, warm years, the rings tend to be wider than the rings in dry, cold years. And a ring might be barely visible if the tree faced a drought.

ROCK ON

Some rocks can also tell a climate tale. Fossils are the remains of ancient organic matter, like plants and animals, that are locked into rocks. Scientists who study fossils say some of these remains show that Earth had an extreme hot period millions of years ago. It lasted for 150,000 years! The fossils of plants and animals that today love warm climates have been found in regions that are now cold. Alligators, for example, which love swampy waters of the southern United States, once lived in the middle of the country and as far north as Canada. Shifts in the tectonic plates under Earth's surface slowly dried up a seaway where the ancient gators lived.

COLD TAKES HOLD

Earth can also have long periods of much cooler temperatures. During these cold times, glaciers and huge sheets of ice move down from the North Pole and cover the land. When that happens, it's called an ice age, and there have been at least five major ones over millions of years. The last ice age in North America ended around 10,000 years ago. Another one might come, but you won't see it—scientists predict it's about 30,000 years away!

THE NOT-SO-LIL' CHILL

Earth's climate can sometimes cool down enough in one area to create a mini-ice age. That's what happened in the beginning of the 14th century in parts of northern Europe and North America. In some places, the average temperature dropped by more than 3°F (1.7°C). The cold killed crops and even caused some glaciers to spread into towns, wiping them out. This "Little Ice Age" lasted in some areas until the middle of the 1800s.

MAP KEY

☐ Ice extent during the last ice age

RUSSIA
Greenland (DENMARK)
ICELAND
Alaska (U.S.A.)
CANADA
PACIFIC OCEAN
UNITED STATES
ATLANTIC OCEAN

ILLUSTRATION OF SNOWBALL EARTH

Did You Know?

"Snowball Earth" describes two time periods about 700 million years ago when almost the whole planet was covered with ice and snow.

Shaping CLIMATE

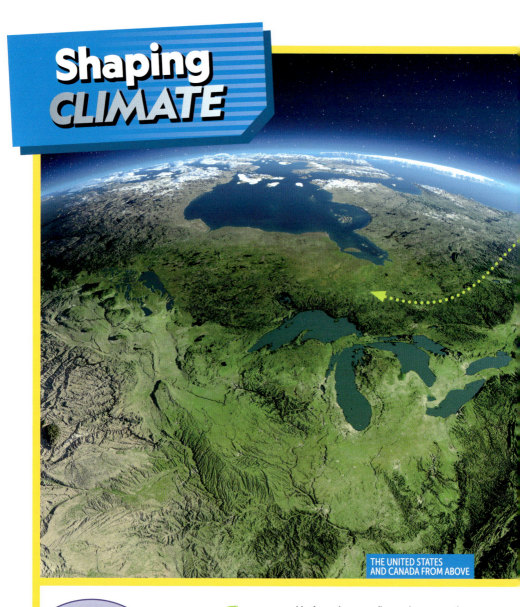

THE UNITED STATES AND CANADA FROM ABOVE

As you read before, there are five major types of climates around the world (see page 10): tropical, with high average temperatures and heavy rains; dry or arid, with little precipitation; temperate, with warm summers, cold winters, and plenty of precipitation all year long; continental, with extreme changes in temperature, from warm summers to really cold winters; and polar, with cold annual average temperatures.

THE BIG FIVE

Factors on land, in the oceans, and in the air shape a region's climate. Here are five major ones:

Latitude: On maps, lines running horizontally indicate a place's latitude. It's measured in degrees, and it shows the spot's distance north or south of the Equator. That distance helps determine if an area is apt to have warm or cold average temperatures.

Elevation: This is the distance that a place sits above sea level. Spots with higher elevation tend to be colder than ones along the coast.

Location: As the sun warms Earth, geographic features can affect temperature. Forests and oceans, for example, soak up some of that heat, so places near them tend to be cooler than a desert or wide open plain.

Ocean Circulation: Parts of the ocean's seawater move around the globe in predictable ways, creating currents. Some ocean currents, like the Gulf Stream, carry warm water, which can affect a region's temperatures. London, England, and Calgary, Canada, are at roughly the same latitude, but England has much warmer average temperatures during the winter. That's partly because of the Gulf Stream.

Atmospheric Circulation: The air in the atmosphere moves in distinct patterns; jet streams are one example (see page 85). But the atmosphere is on the move in other ways, too. Earth's tilt and its massive landforms—its continents—affect how the air moves, which affects climate. For example, air circulation near the Equator carries warm, moist air into the atmosphere, leading to the heavy precipitation in tropical rainforests.

People, plants, and animals have adapted to live in all sorts of climates. But there are limits. At present, people can't live above elevations of 17,500 feet (5,300 m) because it's too hard to grow crops and the air has less oxygen in it. And bitterly cold and windy Antarctica has no permanent residents, although there are permanent bases there that are used for research.

SMALL STUFF

A large climate area can have a smaller climate within it, called a microclimate, with much different temperatures and precipitation. Cities often have higher temperatures than open spaces nearby. That's because buildings and streets soak up the sun's heat. Valleys often have cooler air than higher areas around them because cold air is heavier than warm air and it sinks into the valleys. Knowing the microclimate where you live is important if you and your family grow your own vegetables or like to garden—or just want to be prepared for the weather outside! Even a single mountain can have microclimates, from one side to another or from the ground to its peak.

ARCTIC OCEAN

PACIFIC OCEAN

NORTH AMERICA

EUROPE

ASIA

ATLANTIC OCEAN

AFRICA

PACIFIC OCEAN

MAP KEY
- 🟩 Tropical
- 🟧 Dry
- 🟨 Temperate
- 🟦 Cold
- 🟪 Polar

SOUTH AMERICA

INDIAN OCEAN

AUSTRALIA

SOUTHERN OCEAN

ANTARCTICA

THIS MAP SHOWS THE WORLD'S CLIMATES.

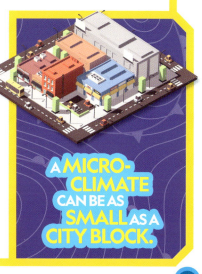

A MICROCLIMATE CAN BE AS SMALL AS A CITY BLOCK.

A Trip to THE TROPICS

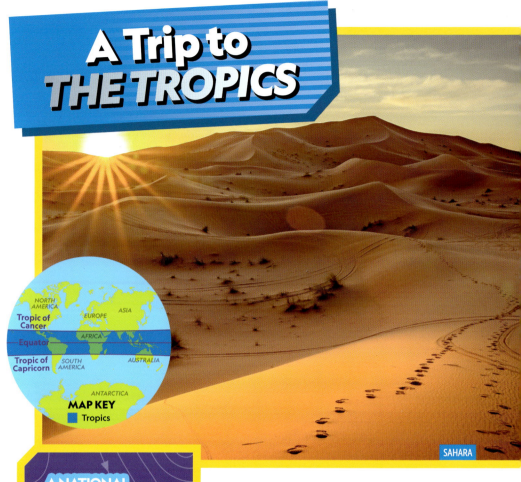

Tropic of Cancer

Equator

Tropic of Capricorn

NORTH AMERICA

EUROPE

ASIA

AFRICA

SOUTH AMERICA

AUSTRALIA

ANTARCTICA

MAP KEY
■ Tropics

SAHARA

A NATIONAL PARK IN THE **TROPICAL RAINFOREST** OF **PERU** HAS **MORE THAN 1,300 KINDS** OF BUTTERFLIES— **TWICE AS MANY** AS IN THE ENTIRE UNITED STATES.

From towering rainforests to the sandy stretches of the Sahara, Earth's tropical climate region has a range of natural features and wildlife. But one thing is true across the tropics—it's hot! Lying on either side of the Equator, this region gets more direct sunlight than the rest of the planet. The lines of latitude that define the tropics are called the Tropic of Cancer, which is north of the Equator, and the Tropic of Capricorn, south of the Equator.

THREE ZONES IN ONE

Large parts of the tropics get heavy rainfall, and the year has just two seasons—wet and dry. The tropical climate area is divided into three smaller areas, or zones, based on how much rain they get. The tropical wet zone is home to the world's tropical rainforests (though there are other kinds of rainforests, too—see page 122). These forests are found along the Equator, and one thing's for sure—you'll know what weather to expect most days. The temperature is always warm and muggy, and rain is common. Some areas might have dry spells, but overall, this tropical zone features a yearly average rainfall between 70 and 100 inches (178 and 254 cm). Hawaii is one example of a tropical rainforest zone.

The second tropical zone is called tropical monsoon. This climate is found mostly in southern Asia and western Africa. Unlike in tropical rainforests, these regions receive most of their rain during the summer. India is particularly known for this climate. Learn more about the upsides and downsides of monsoons on page 106.

Not every part of the tropics gets drenched with rain. The third zone, the savanna, features open grasslands. And unlike the rest of the tropics, it has three seasons: One is cool and dry, one is hot and dry, and the third is hot and wet. Africa's Serengeti, a vast plain, is a famous savanna region (see page 108).

THE RAINY WEATHER IN TROPICAL SRI LANKA HELPS 250 DIFFERENT TYPES OF FROGS THRIVE.

A KNOWN ZONE

The weather closest to the Equator is shaped in part by winds from the Northern and Southern Hemispheres that converge, or meet, there. The winds lift up heat, helping create a string of clouds that can stretch several hundred miles. The clouds cover what's called the intertropical convergence zone. Rains in the zone can be short, but intense, with an inch (2.5 cm) or more falling in just one hour. The area's winds rise into the atmosphere, leaving the ocean's surface calm. Sailors call this region "the doldrums." Sailing ships can find it hard to catch a breeze.

SAVANNA

TROPICAL MONSOON

Rainforest
WONDERS

The tropics are home to the greatest number of living things on the planet. The rainforests alone have as many as 30 million plant and animal species, and new ones are discovered every year.

A HELPFUL HABITAT

Rainforests are good for the planet. They play a big part in the water cycle (see page 24). The plants there soak up water and then release some as vapor, helping create clouds that travel around the world. The plants also pull tons of carbon dioxide out of the air. This gas is one of the sources of global warming.

Some rainforest plants are medical marvels. Indigenous people use them to treat diseases and help wounds heal. Quinine, a drug used to treat malaria, was originally made from the bark of a tropical South American tree.

DANGERS AHEAD

The tropics, though, are losing a lot of their rainforests. In Brazil, Indonesia, and elsewhere, people are cutting them down to provide open land for farming. Some rainforests are destroyed by mining. Governments and private groups are trying to find ways to preserve the rainforests. These include buying land so that companies can't develop it or paying countries to stop cutting down trees.

Is there a shady spot for me?

ONE ACRE (0.4 HA) OF PANAMA'S RAINFOREST HAS MORE THAN 25,000 DIFFERENT SPECIES OF ARTHROPODS—CRITTERS THAT INCLUDE SPIDERS, SCORPIONS, AND BUGS.

A rainforest has different layers. At the tippy-top of the tallest trees in the rainforest is the emergent layer. These trees grow 200 feet (60 m) and higher to reach the sunlight. The animals that live at these heights include bats, birds, and butterflies. Some of the treetop dwellers are gliders, like the sugar glider of Australia and nearby islands. This tiny mammal can glide about 150 feet (45 m) as it goes from one tree to another.

The canopy is the layer below the emergent layer. The treetops here create shade that covers the lower layers. The thick growth of leaves and branches is sometimes called the rainforest's roof. Fruit trees here, such as figs, provide food for the many animals that live in the canopy. Orchids cling to many of the trees, getting the food they need from rain and the air.

The next layer is the understory. It receives a little more light than the floor below it, so more plants can live here. They often have big leaves to soak up as much sun as possible. Animals that live here include tree frogs, jaguars in the jungles of Central and South America, and the green mamba snake of Africa.

At the bottom of the rainforest is the floor. Almost no sunlight reaches the ground through the tall trees above it, so very few plants can live here. Leaves that reach the ground provide food for insects, worms, and other crawly creatures. And they then become a nice meal for animals such as wild pigs and anteaters.

Lots of LIFE

Spiders and lizards and frogs, oh my! These are just some of the interesting critters you might stumble upon in a tropical rainforest.

SETH MACFARLANE'S TORRENT FROG

The name of this frog, discovered in Ecuador in 2018, might seem familiar—Seth is the creator of the *Family Guy* cartoon. The frog was named for him because he's also a defender of rainforest wildlife. It may look cute, but you wouldn't want to pet one. Poison in its skin can make your skin itch for hours.

MATSCHIE'S TREE KANGAROO

Hop over to New Guinea to check out this little cousin of the much bigger 'roos that live in Australia. As its name suggests, the Matschie's tree kangaroo spends most of its time high above the rainforest floor, up 100 feet (30 m) or more in the treetops. It even sleeps in the trees! Its sharp claws give it a good grip, and a long tail helps it keep its balance.

Say "cheese!"

GOLIATH BIRD-EATING SPIDER

Among all spiders, this giant tarantula ranks as the world's biggest. Found in the Amazon of South America, this amazing arachnid can have a leg span of 11 inches (28 cm). It dines mostly on insects, not birds, but frogs and mice can be on the menu, too. The goliath sinks its one-inch (2.5-cm)-long fangs into its meal, then releases a poison. Once the prey is dead, the spider shoots it full of stomach juices that turn the animal's insides into a goopy liquid, which the spider then sucks up.

PARSON'S CHAMELEON

Another record setter that calls the tropics home is the Parson's chameleon. Reaching up to two feet (0.6 m) long, these reptiles are the largest chameleons in the world. They cling to branches in the rainforest of the African nation of Madagascar, where they catch insects with their long tongues. Like other chameleons, they can change color. The Parson's chameleon also has big, bulging eyes that let it see in any direction without turning its head.

AWL TREE

This tree has dozens of names, reflecting the many places where it grows in the tropics and other warm areas. In parts of Africa, it's called a "bumbo" or "bungbo," while people in some Caribbean islands call it "the painkiller." Whatever its name, the tree is famous for its fruit, called noni. To many, it smells like strong cheese or vomit. Maybe that's why the plant is called "forbidden fruit" in the Caribbean country of Barbados. Despite the stinky smell, people have long used the fruit and other parts of the tree as a form of medicine. It's been used to treat everything from mouth infections to swelling in the stomach.

ORCHID MANTIS

Peekaboo!

You have to look closely to spot this sneaky insect—it blends in well with the flower it's named for. With this camouflage, other insects don't have a prayer when this mantis is on the prowl. Bugs that zoom toward the orchid become a meal for the mantis.

Tropic TOPICS

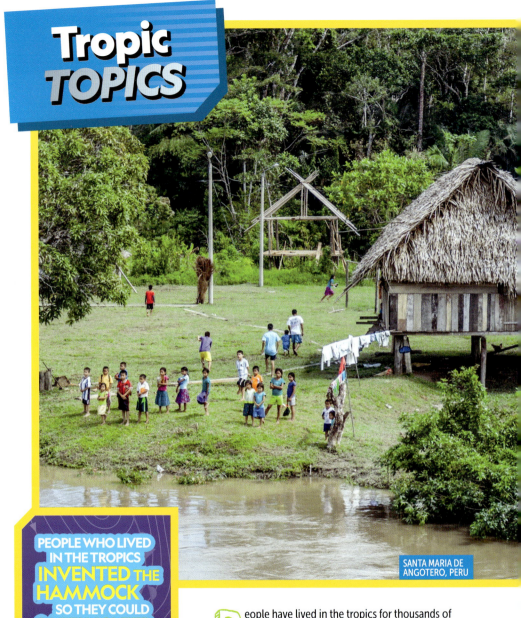

SANTA MARIA DE ANGOTERO, PERU

eople have lived in the tropics for thousands of years. And by 2050, it's estimated that more than half of Earth's population will live in a tropical climate—almost five billion people!

ON THE GROW

In some remote regions of tropical rainforests, about 1.5 million Indigenous people still live as their ancestors did long ago. They survive in what can be a challenging climate. Most feed themselves by hunting, fishing, and gathering crops that grow in the wild. Some people also

A FLOATING HOUSE IN AMAZONAS, BRAZIL

practice shifting agriculture. They clear some land, raise crops there for a few years, then let plants grow wild again as they farm a new area. This kind of farming goes on in the rainforests of South America, Central Africa, and Borneo.

HIGH AND DRY

People who live in the rainforest know that having the right house is important for staying safe. In parts of the rainforest of Brazil, along the Amazon River, that means building your house on a raft. They don't have to worry about rising waters flooding their homes after heavy tropical rains.

Some rainforest dwellers in Africa are nomadic—they move to new locations several times a year. They build dome-shaped homes out of young trees and leaves, under the branches of much taller trees. Those trees provide welcome shade.

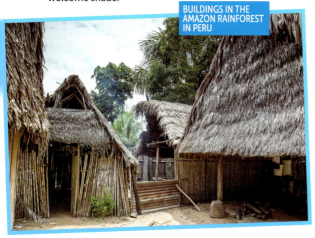
BUILDINGS IN THE AMAZON RAINFOREST IN PERU

TROPICAL TROUBLES

Malaria is one of many common diseases in the tropics. This disease, which causes a fever, chills, and vomiting, is spread by mosquitoes carrying pathogens—tiny living things such as bacteria and viruses. These pathogens love the warm, humid tropical climate. People can get sick by eating or drinking something that contains pathogens. Or insects, like the mosquitoes that transmit malaria, might carry a pathogen and pass it on to people through a bite. Over time, some tropical diseases have spread. People traveling to and from tropical countries might get sick and carry the disease to other areas.

WHERE IN THE WORLD? RAINFOREST EMPIRES

The Aztec, Maya, and Inca were some of the Indigenous people who built great empires in the tropical regions of the Americas before Europeans first arrived. Scientists are still uncovering remains of some of the great cities these people built, such as a Maya city now called Ocomtún. It was discovered in 2023.

SURVIVOR STORIES:
LOST IN THE FOREST

French Guiana, France

ARCTIC OCEAN

NORTH AMERICA
EUROPE
ASIA
PACIFIC OCEAN
AFRICA
INDIAN OCEAN
SOUTH AMERICA
PACIFIC OCEAN
AUSTRALIA
ATLANTIC OCEAN
SOUTHERN OCEAN
ANTARCTICA

LOÏC PILLOIS WITH OFFICIALS IN FRENCH GUIANA

oïc Pillois and Guilhem Nayral were starting to panic. Early in 2007, they had left their homes in France to hike through the rainforest in the South American territory of French Guiana. Now, almost at the end of their trek, they realized they were lost and out of food. They decided to set up a camp, rather than risking getting more lost in the thick forest. A tarp kept them dry when rains came.

LOÏC PILLOIS

A PAINFUL MEAL

Using a lighter that Pillois had, they started a fire, hoping any rescuers searching for them would see it. But the rainforest canopy was too thick for anyone to spot them from the air. For food, the men turned to small jungle animals, such as insects, frogs, and a turtle. They even caught and ate two tarantulas. They burned off the hairs on the spider's legs, which can sting. But for their second tarantula meal, they didn't burn off all the hairs. Nayral took a bite and immediately had severe pain. Because Nayral was already weak from a lack of food, Pillois thought his friend needed immediate help. He set off to try to find someone.

RESCUED!

Pillois searched for Saül, the town where he and Nayral had planned to end their hike. After almost two days, he stumbled into the town. Officials there sent a helicopter to find Nayral. Given his health, he might not have survived much longer in the rainforest. Altogether, the two hikers had spent 51 days in the rainforest. Nayral had lost more than 50 pounds (23 kg), while Pillois had dropped more than 30 (14 kg).

STAYING SAFE

Ian Craddock was a guide who led people through the rainforests of Guyana, a country near French Guiana. After hearing the story of Loïc Pillois and Guilhem Nayral, he shared some tips for anyone planning to hike through the jungle:

- Use a local guide, or at least do plenty of research using local sources before heading out.
- Cell phones won't work in remote areas, so take some other device that has GPS and some sort of radio to communicate. Pillois and Nayral had neither.
- Carry a fishing kit.
- Carry special flares that emit smoke that can rise above the forest canopy.

DIGGING IN

The tarantula wasn't the only rainforest dweller that troubled Nayral. Small worms dug into both his and Pillois's skin. The worms were parasites—harmful creatures that survive by living on or in other creatures and getting their food from these hosts. Parasites are common in the tropics, and malaria is one of the diseases they cause.

Monsoon SEASON

Time to put on your rain boots, people!

A FLOODED ROAD IN BANGKOK, THAILAND

During monsoon season in East Asia, which spans from April to September every year, some of the world's heaviest rains occur. "Monsoon" refers to changes in the direction of the strongest winds in an area. Those shifts bring rains that can cause deadly floods. But let's look at how those rains can also be helpful.

SUMMER SATURATION

The switch in wind direction comes as the seasons change. In and near part of the Asian tropics, monsoon season usually begins in April, with warm, moist air coming off the Indian Ocean. As the air rolls over land, the humidity goes up and the rain comes down, falling on India, Pakistan, and nearby nations. The rain usually lasts until September.

FARMERS IN WEST BENGAL, INDIA

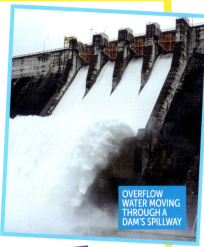
OVERFLOW WATER MOVING THROUGH A DAM'S SPILLWAY

Monster monsoon rains fell in this region during the late spring and summer of 2022. Several hundred people died during floods and landslides, and in the nation of Bangladesh, hundreds of thousands fled their homes.

Despite the destructive power of the monsoon rains, they play an important weather role. Farmers rely on them to water crops and keep farm animals alive. The increased rain also helps create hydroelectric power—electricity created by the energy of water rushing through special dams.

WINTER WINDS, TOO

Other parts of Asia feel the effects of a winter monsoon. From October to April, these winds blow in from the northeast. The Himalaya, a massive mountain range that crosses parts of India, Nepal, and several countries that border them, block some moisture from reaching the other side of the range. That creates dry conditions in some parts of India—so dry that they face droughts. But the winter monsoon brings rain farther east, in the countries of Indonesia and Malaysia.

DESERT RAINS

Part of North America has a monsoon season, too. It usually starts at the end of June or beginning of July and lasts through September, as warm air from the Gulf of California mixes with warm air from the Gulf of Mexico over the Sierra Madre Occidental, a mountain chain in Mexico. The air brings rain, hail, and thunderstorms to parts of Mexico and the U.S. states of Arizona, New Mexico, and Texas. These storms tend to have short bursts of precipitation in the afternoon and evening. They can cause flash floods in ditches, called arroyos or washes, that are usually dry. But the North American monsoon also waters crops and can help firefighters put out wildfires.

UNITED STATES
Arizona
New Mexico
Texas
Sierra Madre Occidental
Gulf of California
PACIFIC OCEAN
MEXICO
Gulf of Mexico

MAP KEY
Monsoon region

AN APPROACHING MONSOON IN ARIZONA

Great GRASSLAND

AFRICAN BUSH ELEPHANTS IN SERENGETI NATIONAL PARK, TANZANIA

I'm on a roll!

ONE PART OF THE SERENGETI HAS MORE THAN 100 SPECIES OF DUNG BEETLES—INSECTS THAT COLLECT AND STORE OTHER CREATURES' POOP, WHICH BABY DUNG BEETLES EAT!

Not all regions with tropical climates are wet and humid most of the year. One area has two distinct dry seasons to go along with one long period of rain. This tropical climate is called savanna, and that's also the name given to the grasslands often found in this climate. The savanna is warm and dry for up to half the year, but during the wet season, when it rains, it pours. Some savannas see more than four feet (1.2 m) of rain during that period.

SERENGETI SAVANNAS

Every continent except Antarctica has some savanna regions. But Africa takes the crown for having the most—almost half the continent is covered with the grasslands commonly found in the tropical wet and dry regions. And Africa's best known savanna region is the Serengeti. Its fame comes from the variety of animals that live there.

These African animal all-stars include the African savanna elephant—the largest land mammal on the continent. (A smaller cousin is found in some African forests.) Another is the rhino—one species of this big beast can weigh almost 6,000 pounds (2,700 kg). Towering over parts of the Serengeti are giraffes, which like to nibble on the leaves of tall trees. These three animals are all

TWO GIRAFFES IN OKAVANGO, BOTSWANA

herbivores, meaning they only eat plants. They share the plant buffet with zebras, wildebeests, hippos, and a host of others.

Those plant-eaters sometimes end up as a meal for the Serengeti's cunning carnivores— lions, leopards, cheetahs, and hyenas. The cheetah is famous for its speed, which can hit about 70 miles an hour (110 km/h) in short bursts. Lions and hyenas often compete for the same prey, and they sometimes kill each other's young.

CLIMATE CHALLENGES

The shifting wet and dry seasons can make life tough for some savanna dwellers. Water and some kinds of plants can be hard to find during the dry season, so some animals have to cover a lot of ground searching for it. Each year, about two million wildebeests make what's called the Great Migration, an almost 500-mile (805-km) hunt for grass. Lightning during the dry season can spark wildfires, but the blazes are actually helpful. Birds can easily feast on insects and other animals killed by the flames. And grasses that burn have deep roots, which soon send up new, tender shoots for animals to graze.

Did You Know?

The baobab tree survives the dry season by storing water in its trunk—up to 26,000 gallons (100,000 L). Elephants sometimes rip open the trees to get to the water inside.

WILDEBEESTS IN THE AFRICAN SAVANNA

109

Cutting-Edge CLIMATE SCIENCE

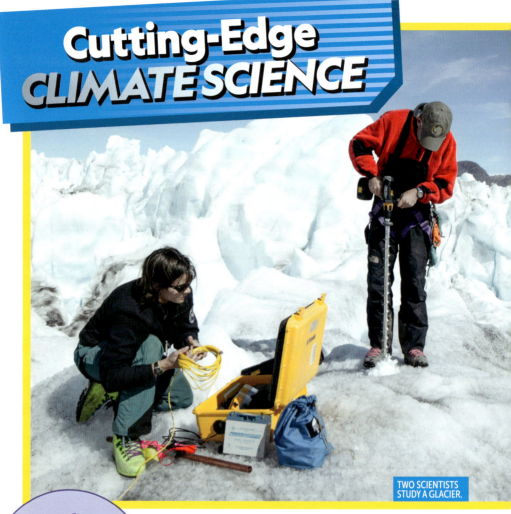

TWO SCIENTISTS STUDY A GLACIER.

Did You Know?

Working together, two supercomputers that NOAA climatologists use can perform 29 quadrillion calculations every second. That's 29 followed by 15 zeros!

IBM SUPERCOMPUTERS

We wouldn't know as much as we do about Earth's climate without some special scientists. Climatologists study weather patterns and changes in the atmosphere over time. They want to understand how natural and human forces shape the climate.

As with meteorology (see Aristotle sidebar on page 71), people have wondered for thousands of years what shapes the weather and climate. But modern science has greatly aided climatologists in their work. The tools they now rely on include satellites, powerful supercomputers, and stations that automatically record weather data 24 hours a day.

With the knowledge they gain, climate experts can make predictions about long-term weather patterns. These predictions can help people prepare for drought conditions and estimate how much energy they might need during periods of extreme hot or cold temperatures.

DURING EL NIÑO YEARS, WARM SURFACE WATER SPREADS INTO EASTERN PARTS OF THE PACIFIC OCEAN, AFFECTING WEATHER AND SEA LIFE AROUND THE GLOBE.

CHARTING CHANGE

One focus of climatologists is studying weather patterns in a particular region—for example, what are the normal conditions that create a tropical climate versus a polar one? They also look at cause and effect. For example, how does sunlight affect temperature? And climatologists are particularly concerned with changes over time. Climatologists were the first to see the connection between human activity, such as using fuels that create greenhouse gases, and global warming (see page 144).

Part of their work involves studying how changes in air and ocean currents affect weather. Climatologists have learned that two distinct patterns in the Pacific Ocean greatly affect world weather. A change in the direction of some winds near the Equator creates El Niño climate conditions. El Niño warms part of the ocean and brings increased rainfall to the southern United States and drier conditions to the north. La Niña, which leads to colder Pacific waters, has the opposite effect on rainfall.

A RESEARCHER EXTRACTING A SAMPLE OF ICE

WEATHER HERO: FOCUSED ON FIRE

In 2019, Australian climatologist Julie Arblaster saw some dangerous signs in the data she studied. An El Niño was underway in the Pacific Ocean, and average temperatures were both higher and lower than normal in different parts of the Indian Ocean. Additionally, Arblaster and other scientists she worked with saw that the polar vortex over Antarctica was weakening. To Arblaster, all those climatic conditions meant that Australia would be hotter and drier than usual in the coming spring, which starts in September in Australia, and that raised the risk of destructive wildfires. Fires did break out, destroying 3,000 homes and killing billions of animals. Through her work, Arblaster showed that a weakening polar vortex could help predict the dry conditions that helped fuel wildfires.

My, IT'S DRY

I should have brought a bigger canteen!

A CLIFF IN THE GOBI, ASIA

LONG-EARED JERBOA

We think of deserts as super dry, hot places. But in some deserts, temperatures can plunge to minus double digits! So, if it's not the heat, what makes a desert a desert?

RUNNING HOT AND COLD

Technically speaking, a desert is any region that receives less than 10 inches (25 cm) of rain each year. Scientists divide deserts into three smaller categories: cold arid, hot arid, and steppe.

Temperatures in cold arid climates, which usually have higher altitudes than hot arid regions, can get chilly, especially in winter. For example, Central Asia's Gobi desert can see temperatures plunge to −40°F (−40°C)! Meanwhile, summers in this region can see temperatures hit 75°F (24°C) or more.

MAP KEY
■ Cold desert climate

Most cold arid climate regions sit at latitudes between 20° and 35° north and south of the Equator. They often have mountains along their western edge, which block precipitation from reaching them. That's the case in parts of the U.S. states of Wyoming, which is east of the Rocky Mountains, and Nevada, which is east of the Sierra Nevada.

The cold arid climate can be tough on wildlife. The lack of water limits which plants and animals can thrive there. And people who raise livestock can see harsh winter weather. But some animals still call these cold arid regions home, including snow leopards, which live in mountainous parts of Central Asia, and a small rodent called the jerboa, which looks a bit like a cross between a rabbit, mouse, and kangaroo. Like many small animals in arid areas, this mammal spends a lot of time in holes in the ground. It uses different burrows in different ways, including ones to beat the heat and others for winter hibernation.

A REAL DUST-UP

Dust or sandstorms are a hazard in many parts of the world, but especially in arid zones. With little or no precipitation, strong winds of 75 miles an hour (121 km/h) or more stir up immense sandstorms. One that started in the Gobi in 2006 blew tons of sand into the Chinese capital of Beijing, carrying the sand more than 1,000 miles (1,610 km). In 2021, a series of sandstorms in the Gobi killed more than one million farm animals in Mongolia. To prevent Gobi sands from reaching parts of China, the country has planted more than 66 billion trees across almost 3,000 miles (4,800 km) to block the storms. The trees form China's "Great Green Wall."

SNOW LEOPARD

CAMELS IN THE GOBI, DUNHUANG, CHINA

Hot ZONES

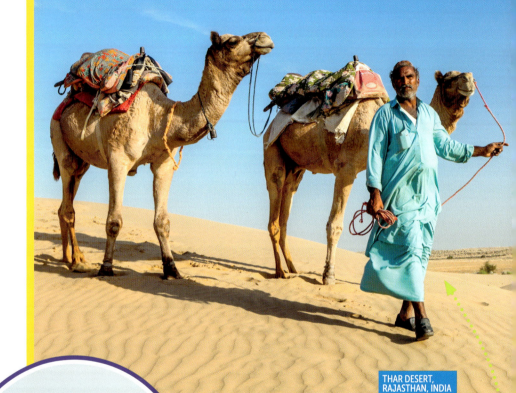

THAR DESERT, RAJASTHAN, INDIA

A TENT IN THE SAHARA, AFRICA

If you really want to turn up the heat, head to one of the world's hot arid regions. Little precipitation and plenty of sunshine combine to make these the hottest places on Earth. During some months, however, nighttime temperatures can fall, thanks to what's called radiational cooling. Heat absorbed by the ground during the day drifts upward under a cloudless nighttime sky.

HOME IN THE HEAT

People find a way to survive in some of the world's hottest climates. How do they adapt to extreme heat? One way is by wearing the right clothes. For example, long, flowing robes and dresses let air move around the body while

AMAZING ANIMALS

One of the most famous arid-area animals is the camel, which has uniquely adapted to life in the desert. Most camels have one hump, but ones found in cold arid regions have two. Camels can go for a week without water, and thanks to the fat they store in their humps, they can go even longer without food. They're strong, too—they can carry a person or goods for about 20 miles (32 km) every day, even in the hottest conditions.

helping keep off the sun. Desert dwellers have traditionally done the same thing with their homes. They set up tents that provide shade and also let in breezes.

Some people rely on technology to help them survive in deserts. Modern buildings have air-conditioning, and plentiful sunlight can sometimes provide the solar energy to keep things cool. People living in hot arid regions also need plenty of water. In the desert Southwest of the United States, millions of people use water provided by rivers, collected in dams, and sent to cities and towns by pipes.

BY THE NUMBERS

BEAT THIS HEAT!

Highest daytime temperature:
Furnace Creek, California, 134°F (56.7°C)

Highest overnight low temperature:
Khasab Airport, Oman, 111.6°F (44.2°C)

Hottest one hour at night:
Death Valley National Park, 120°F (48.9°C)

Highest average temperature:
Dallol, Ethiopia, 94°F (34.4°C)

WHERE IN THE WORLD? IN A FOG

Arid regions get little rain, but nothing beats the dry spells of Chile's Atacama Desert. The Andes mountains to the east block some rain, and cool Pacific waters to the west keep seawater from evaporating, so few rain clouds form there. The Atacama is not a particularly hot desert, but some regions have gone years without rain. When precipitation does come, it's usually in the form of fog rolling in from the ocean. People along the coast set up nets to collect the fog to use as drinking water. One net can trap up to 106 gallons (400 L) of water each day.

ATACAMA DESERT

Steppe *LIVELY*

MONGOLIAN STEPPE

Long stretches of short grasses define arid areas called steppes. The climate there is called semiarid, since these regions get more precipitation than the other arid zones, but not as much as other climates. On average, a steppe receives between 10 and 20 inches (25 and 50 cm) of rain each year.

Steppes are usually found on high, flat stretches of land called plateaus. They have few trees, except near bodies of water. With their grassy fields, steppes provide good food for grazing animals, as in the Great Plains in the middle of the United States. The more rain a steppe gets, the taller its grasses grow.

ACROSS TWO CONTINENTS

Climatologists divide the steppes into hot and cold semiarid areas. While the cold regions can have warm summers, they have much colder winters than the hot steppes. One of the cold semiarid steppes is the Eurasian Steppe, which goes from Hungary in Europe across Central Asia. Over the centuries, people from Central Asia have moved westward through the steppe to settle in the Middle East and parts of Europe.

MAP KEY
Eurasian Steppe

RUSSIA

HUNGARY
UKRAINE
MOLDOVA — Crimea
ROMANIA — Black Sea
Caspian Sea
KAZAKHSTAN
MONGOLIA
CHINA
PACIFIC OCEAN

STEPPE-ING UP THE HEAT

Steppe regions described as hot semiarid are usually close to regions with a tropical climate. Their summers can be very hot, with cool but not cold winters. Most hot steppes are found in South Asia, Africa, and Australia. Parts of Australia's outback have this climate. Australia's steppe lands are home to the emu, the world's second largest bird. To spot one, don't look to the sky—emus can't fly!

ON FOOT, EMUS CAN RACE ALONG AT SPEEDS OF UP TO 30 MILES AN HOUR (48 KM/H).

WAYBACK WEATHER: A REIGN FROM RAIN

Rain rules!

Nomadic people have lived on the steppes of Mongolia for thousands of years. They raise livestock on the cold, dry, grassy lands, surviving despite the lack of precipitation. But for one period more than 800 years ago, rain fell there as it hadn't fallen in perhaps centuries. The temperature rose, too. And those brief changes in the climate helped build one of the greatest empires the world has known. The wet, warm weather meant there was plenty of grass to feed Mongol sheep, goats, and other livestock—including their warhorses. That let a Mongol leader named Genghis Khan build an army that could fight and defeat neighboring tribes. Genghis, his sons, and his grandsons went on to defeat armies across Eurasia. The rain wasn't the only reason the Mongols conquered so much of the world. On their horses, they were extremely skilled fighters. But the record rains seemed to play a part in helping them thrive.

Walk on the MILD SIDE

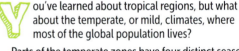

You've learned about tropical regions, but what about the temperate, or mild, climates, where most of the global population lives?

Parts of the temperate zones have four distinct seasons, while others have less variety. A location's latitude and distance from large bodies of water shape the climate particulars. But just because it's called "mild" doesn't mean you won't feel the heat during the summer or need a coat in winter! Here are the ins and outs of temperate climates.

FAIR—AND RARE

One temperate climate is called Mediterranean, like the sea of the same name. Spots along the coast of that body of water have warm, dry summers and short, not-too-cold winters—just two major seasons. The cooler temps also bring rain. Outside of the Mediterranean region, this climate is rare. It's only found between the latitudes of 30° and 40° on the west coast of continents: part of Chile, Baja California in Mexico, most of California, two locations in Australia, and one in South Africa.

THE GOLDEN GATE BRIDGE, SAN FRANCISCO, CALIFORNIA, U.S.A.

FOGGED IN

Along the Mediterranean Sea, the mild weather led people thousands of years ago to settle near the coast. They could easily grow crops there for most of the year and not shiver during the winter. Today, the Mediterranean regions are great for growing such crops as citrus fruit, grapes, nuts, olives, and many kinds of vegetables. Overall, these regions have a great diversity of plant and animal life, second only to tropical rainforests.

The coastal areas in some Mediterranean climate regions don't always see the hot summers that usually define the climate. The California city of San Francisco is one good example. This hilly city is famous for its summer fog, which keeps temperatures cool. The fog forms because of chilly ocean currents that stream down from Alaska, combined with cold waters farther out in the Pacific Ocean. As the temperatures warm over land, fog rolls in from the water. While the fog might make for cool summers and block your view of San Francisco's famous Golden Gate Bridge, it is helpful. For several months of the year, it provides much of the water for California's immense redwood trees. The water also drips down from the trees, giving a needed drink to tiny creatures that live on the forest floor.

THE AMALFI COAST, ITALY

Sticky SUMMERS

I'm melting!

SYDNEY HARBOUR, SYDNEY, AUSTRALIA

Just because a region is considered temperate doesn't mean it doesn't get extreme weather. One temperate climate, called humid subtropical, is often in the path of tropical cyclones, hurricanes, and tornadoes. This climate area is found on the southeastern coast of every continent except Antarctica. In the United States and China, it can extend farther inland.

The humid subtropical climate features an extended summer season of hot and humid weather, similar to

SAVANNAH, GEORGIA, U.S.A.

SHANGHAI, CHINA

FITTING THE BILL

A really unique animal called the duck-billed platypus can be found in the humid subtropical regions of Australia. This animal is just one of two mammals on Earth that lay eggs. It has no teeth. As its name suggests, its long snout looks a bit like a duck's bill, and it has webbed front limbs, sort of like a duck's webbed feet. At the rear, the platypus has a flat tail similar to a beaver—and like a beaver, the platypus spends a lot of time in water. Its thick fur helps keep it warm. The male platypus is one of the few mammals that has venom, which it uses to defend itself.

what's found in tropical regions. Temperatures above 90°F (32°C) are common. The nighttime doesn't help people beat the heat because the thermometer doesn't drop much and humid air stays in place. Winters are short and relatively mild—temperatures during this season average between 40°F and 50°F (4°C and 10°C). Some places, though, might see frost. Rain tends to fall evenly throughout the year. Some cities that have a humid subtropical climate are Savannah, Georgia, U.S.A.; Sydney, Australia; and Shanghai, China.

WHERE IN THE WORLD?
DEEP FREEZE

Florida, U.S.A., is the Sunshine State, home to beaches galore. Its climate is a perfect example of a humid subtropical climate—and of how typical climate conditions don't always hold true. When a powerful wintertime low-pressure system moves out, a strong high-pressure system might follow. That one-two punch results in plunging temperatures and strong winds. During the winter of 1894–95, Florida experienced what's been called the "Great Freeze." Two different severe cold spells brought temperatures into the teens, which killed off some of the state's citrus trees. After losing their crops, many citrus farmers moved their businesses farther south, to a warmer part of Florida. Another deep freeze in 1899 led to the lowest temperature reading ever in the state: −2°F (−19°C) in the capital of Tallahassee.

A LOT OF CITRUS, LIKE THESE ORANGES, WAS RUINED DURING THE GREAT FREEZE.

Green SCENE

SEATTLE, WASHINGTON, U.S.A.

OPEN UP TO ARTS

In honor of the rainy climate in Seattle, Washington, U.S.A, the city named a yearly arts festival after a bumbershoot—another name for an umbrella. Bumbershoot features local artists and musicians from the region and across the United States.

One temperate climate, called marine west coast or oceanic climate, is found along the west coasts of continents, as well as some eastern coastal regions. The marine west coast climate is found in regions that sit between 40° and 55° latitudes north and south of the Equator. That includes part of northwestern North America, northwestern Europe, some coasts of South America, and the Pacific islands of New Zealand and Tasmania. So what is it exactly?

STORMY WEATHER

The places with marine west coast climates tend to have cool summers and mild winters, with temperatures that usually don't get too hot or too cold. They also tend to have a lot of cloudy and rainy days. The rain isn't always hard, but it's apt to drizzle for days in a row, and in some places, it might

KERRY, IRELAND

rain more than 150 days per year. All that rain helps keep the landscape in oceanic regions very green, especially in the temperate rainforests that are found only in this climate.

Massive streams of air and water shape some of the conditions in the oceanic climate. High above the ground, the polar jet stream pushes storms eastward toward land during fall, winter, and early spring. In the Atlantic Ocean, the warm waters of the Gulf Stream help keep winter temperatures in Ireland and the United Kingdom higher than they are at other places with the same latitude. It can snow in regions with this climate, but it's rare.

DUBLIN, IRELAND, DOESN'T USUALLY SEE BIG SNOWS, BUT A SERIES OF STORMS IN 1947 LED TO SNOWDRIFTS UP TO 20 FEET (6 M) DEEP! THAT'S TALLER THAN MOST GIRAFFES!

SLOW GROWING

Some of the oldest living things on Earth can be found in the temperate rainforest of Tasmania. The Huon pine is found only in that part of Australia and can reach the ripe old age of 3,000 years! The pine can grow to a height of up to 130 feet (40 m). But its trunk grows bigger by just the smallest amount each year—only a tiny fraction of an inch. Most Huon pines have been cut down for their lumber, which doesn't rot easily and naturally resists pests. But in 2022, a team of environmentalists discovered a new grove of Huon pines, which they believe should be preserved and not cut down.

Reasons for
THE SEASONS

BRØGGER GLACIERS,
SVALBARD, NORWAY

IN SVALBARD, NORWAY, THE SUN DOESN'T SET BETWEEN APRIL 20 AND AUGUST 22.

If you live in most parts of the United States, you know all about the four seasons: winter, spring, summer, and fall (or autumn). The U.S. has many of the different types of temperate climates. There isn't the bitter cold like in the polar regions or the extreme heat and humidity of the tropics. But what gives the temperate regions those four distinct seasons?

WHAT A TRIP

You read a bit about Earth's tilt on page 13. That tilt and Earth's yearly orbit around the sun create the four seasons found in many climates. For part of that orbit, the top part of Earth tips a little bit closer to the sun. That creates summer weather in the Northern Hemisphere. At the same time that it's summer in the northern half of the planet, it's winter in the Southern Hemisphere. The bottom part of Earth is tilting away from the sun.

When summer comes to the Northern Hemisphere, the North Pole is as close as it will get to the sun. That means the sun never sets for several months! The opposite happens at the South Pole, where it remains dark as night for months at a time. The tropical regions near the Equator are always about the same distance from the sun, meaning they get the same amount of sunlight all year long.

As Earth makes its orbit around the sun, the location of summer and winter switch. The Southern Hemisphere's summer starts in December, just as winter is starting in the north.

EQUINOX TALK

On two days of the year, the Northern and Southern Hemispheres get almost equal amounts of sunlight. Those days are known as the equinoxes. The vernal equinox takes place around March 20 and marks the start of spring in the north and fall in the south. The autumnal equinox occurs around September 22, when fall starts in the north and spring starts in the south. Winter and summer have special days that mark their start, too. The summer solstice falls around June 20, when the Northern Hemisphere gets the most amount of sunlight for the year. The winter solstice arrives around December 21 and has the least amount of sunlight. The names of the summer and winter solstices refer to when the seasons start in the Northern Hemisphere.

A LABORATORY IN ANTARCTICA

ANCIENT PEOPLE BUILT SOME STRUCTURES SO THAT CERTAIN POINTS ON THEM LINE UP WITH THE SUN ON THE SUMMER AND WINTER SOLSTICES. ENGLAND'S STONEHENGE, BUILT ABOUT 5,000 YEARS AGO, IS ONE EXAMPLE.

Completely CONTINENTAL

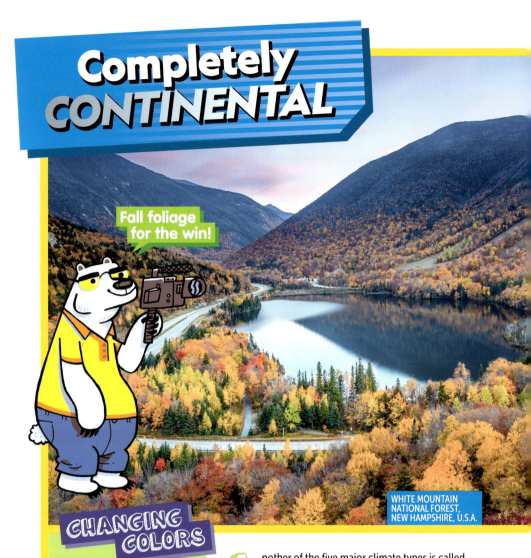

Fall foliage for the win!

WHITE MOUNTAIN NATIONAL FOREST, NEW HAMPSHIRE, U.S.A.

CHANGING COLORS

The weather in the humid continental zones helps determine if fall leaf colors are going to be fantastic or a bit of a flop. The best colors come after a summer with warm days and cooler nights. This combination seems to have the most effect on the plant chemicals that produce shades of red and purple. The amount of moisture in the ground can also affect the color or the timing of when the leaves start to turn. Lots of precipitation in the spring helps bring strong colors. Dry summers can delay the start of the turning.

Another of the five major climate types is called continental. This climate is usually found in the interior of continents, away from the coasts. It has two major divisions, based on geography and temperature. The continental zones are found between temperate and polar climate regions, and are marked by four distinct seasons.

STICKY BUSINESS

One type of continental climate is called humid continental. It's usually further divided into smaller zones, based on the average temperature. This climate is mostly found in the Northern Hemisphere. The continents in the Southern Hemisphere don't have the large landmasses and the right latitude that help create this climate. Large parts of central and eastern Europe and North America have a humid continental climate.

Summers can be sticky with humid air, and winters can be long and cold. Precipitation usually falls throughout the year, though summers can be especially rainy. The weather in the humid continental regions can be extreme. Thunderstorms and tornadoes pop up, wildfires can break out, and winter can bring blizzards. But for leaf peepers, the fall weather can bring an explosion of colors, as leaves turn before they fall off their trees.

HUMID AIR TRAPS ODORS, CAUSING SMELLS TO TRAVEL FARTHER AND LINGER LONGER THAN DRIER AIR. TRASH DAY PLUS HOT, HUMID AIR EQUALS EXTRA PUNGENT.

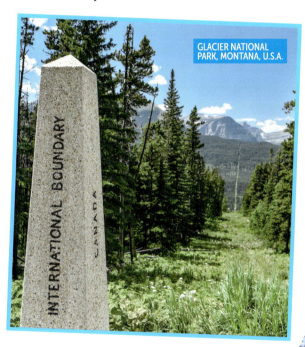

GLACIER NATIONAL PARK, MONTANA, U.S.A.

INTERNATIONAL BOUNDARY

CANADA

WAYBACK WEATHER: A GENERAL'S WINTRY WOES

Too cold! Turn back!

Large parts of Russia have a humid continental climate. The brutal winters that can hit there played a role in shaping world history. French general Napoleon Bonaparte created an empire that stretched across much of western Europe. In 1812, he led his army of more than 500,000 troops into Russia. He took the capital, Moscow, but then decided he couldn't hold the city and began to retreat. The winter solstice was still weeks away, but the temperatures were already dropping fast, and they would hit −13°F (−25°C) before the end of November. The freezing weather and the Russian army reduced Napoleon's forces so badly that only about 112,000 of the troops survived the effort to take Russia. Napoleon's failure there led more European countries to unite to defeat him.

Substantially
COLD

BANFF NATIONAL PARK, ALBERTA, CANADA

orth of the humid continental areas of Europe and North America are the coldest places on Earth outside of the polar regions of Antarctica and the Arctic. These regions have a continental climate called subarctic. ("Sub" means "under" or "below," so the name basically means "under the Arctic.") Places with a subarctic climate include most of the northern parts of Alaska, Canada, Scandinavia, and Russia. The subarctic climate is found only in the Northern Hemisphere.

Not much precipitation falls in these regions, and the coldest winter month can see average temperatures drop to −36°F (−38°C). Places with a subarctic climate see a wide range of temperatures between summer and winter averages—as much as 100°F (55.5°C) in some parts of Siberia.

EVERGREEN SCENE

Even with cold temperatures, the forests of the subarctic regions are teeming with wildlife. Many of these forests are

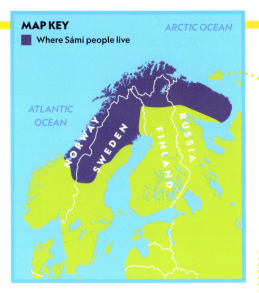

THE SÁMI PEOPLE

Parts of the subarctic region of Scandinavia and Russia are the homeland of an Indigenous people called Sámi. It is estimated that 50,000 to 100,000 Sámi live in that region, with most in Norway. The Sámi adapted to the harsh weather of the area by raising reindeer. The animals pulled sleighs and provided meat, leather, and even milk. Some Sámi still keep reindeer herds, but many now make their living fishing, farming, and taking care of tourists who come to see reindeer and the traditional Sámi way of life.

called taigas or boreal forests. They are filled with conifers—trees that keep their seeds in cones that fall to the ground. Conifers also have needles instead of leaves. The needles don't fall like leaves do, so these trees are also called evergreens. The needles resist the wind, which helps prevent damage to the limbs. And conifers are able to soak up the sun all year long, which helps them make the food they need to live.

In and around the conifer forests live some big mammals, such as moose, caribou, and bears. Other wildlife include the big cats called lynx, great gray owls, and gray wolves. In the summer, a walk through the forest might be a bit buggy, as swarms of mosquitoes come out in the warm weather. They breed in ponds that were frozen during the winter. The bothersome bugs feast on any mammals they can find. But other subarctic critters, such as birds and other insects, feast on the pesky pests.

A REINDEER'S FUR INSULATES THE ANIMAL'S BODY SO WELL AGAINST THE COLD THAT FALLING SNOW WON'T MELT WHEN IT LANDS ON THE REINDEER'S BACK.

Animals' Cool ADAPTATIONS

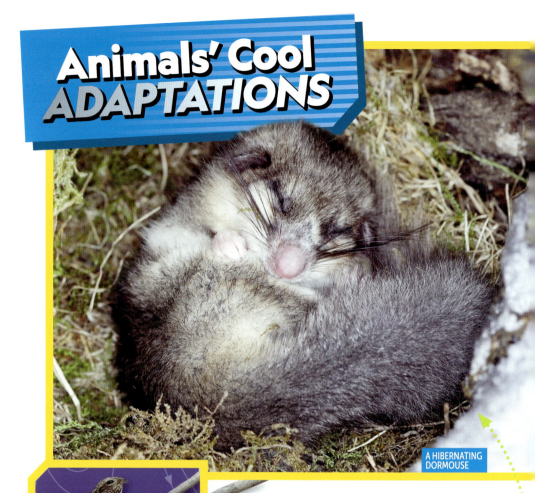

A HIBERNATING DORMOUSE

THE COMMON POORWILL IS THE ONLY BIRD THAT HIBERNATES. THE HOPI PEOPLE OF THE SOUTHWESTERN UNITED STATES CALL IT "THE SLEEPING ONE."

You can adapt to cold winter weather by putting on a coat or simply heading inside. Animals in temperate and colder climates have found their own ways to adapt to winter.

SLOW DOWN!

For many animals, the key to surviving freezing temperatures and a lack of food is to enter a state called dormancy. That often means finding a safe spot and sleeping away most of the winter. Some animals, such as bears, eat a lot before winter hits and then live off the fat stored in their bodies. Other animals, such as squirrels, stock up on food that they bring to their homes.

One form of dormancy is hibernation. True hibernators see their body temperatures fall, their heartbeats go down, and their metabolisms slow, which means they use less energy to live. Bears are not true hibernators because their body temperatures don't drop. But some rodents, such as chipmunks, are true hibernators. So are some bats and hedgehogs.

COLD-BLOODED SLEEP

Cold-blooded animals, such as reptiles and amphibians, have their own kind of dormancy, called brumation. They seek warm spots, such as holes in the ground or gaps in rocks. Some alligators go to sleep under ice that forms on the water's surface. Just their noses stick out, so they can keep breathing while they slumber. Once winter hits, snakes and other reptiles can go for months without eating. Some groups of snakes will seek the same spot for the winter, becoming brumate roommates!

ON THE MOVE

For some animal fliers and swimmers, one common way to deal with winter is to leave it. These animals migrate. Many whales seek cold water in the summer, loading up on food. Then they head for warmer waters during winter to mate and have babies. Migrating birds also head for warmer climates during winter. Some birds travel thousands of miles—some of them flying by night and day for more than a week straight. Some even hoof it—Adélie penguins walk some 8,000 miles (13,000 km) in their migratory trek across Antarctica. They travel from one area where they breed to other locations to search for food, then back again.

ANNUAL MIGRATION OF ADÉLIE PENGUINS

Who you calling beefy?

WHERE IN THE WORLD?
BEEFY BEARS

Each year in early fall, people around the world get to vote for the fattest bear in Alaska's Katmai National Park and Preserve. Starting in June, cameras record the activity of the park's big brown bears, which pack on the pounds as they prepare to hibernate. The biggest male bears weigh more than 1,000 pounds (454 kg) by the time they're ready for their big sleep. As of 2023, bear 480, nicknamed Otis, held the record for most wins in the contest, taking the fat-bear crown four times.

Polar
OPPOSITES

GRAY REINDEER LICHEN

Saving the coldest for last, the final major climate type is named for the North and South Poles. The polar climate is divided into two types: tundra and ice cap. Here's what it's like and what lives there.

TON O' TUNDRA TIDBITS

The tundra describes a climate found at high latitudes and elevations. Winters are long and cold, with average temperatures below freezing for up to 10 months every year. But at least two months a year, the temperature gets above freezing long enough to melt snow. The snow is not deep, as tundra regions are almost desert-like. Some rain falls during the summer, and the cool temperatures keep it from quickly evaporating. Plants use that moisture to live. Many plants grow in groups to stay warm in winter. Flowers

Check out my nifty nose warmer!

usually grow low to the ground to avoid strong winds and extreme cold.

Not many trees grow in the tundra, but moss and lichen adapt well to the cold, dry weather. Lichen are like plants, but they are a combination of other life-forms—a fungus with either algae or bacteria. They're a tasty treat for some of the tundra animals, such as hares, caribou, and moose. And some birds of the region use lichen for their nests.

Indigenous people of Alaska and other tundra regions have traditionally turned to the sea for many of their resources. They hunted whales, walruses, and seals for food and used sealskins for clothing and shelter.

THE VALLEY OF TJÄKTJAVAGGE, KUNGSLEDEN, SWEDEN

ROCK-SOLID SOIL

Tundra regions are mostly covered with frozen soil called permafrost. It can form on land or under oceans—any place where the temperature stays at or below freezing for two or more years. Some permafrost has been frozen for thousands of years. During summer, the top few inches thaw enough to let plants grow.

Scientists are concerned because some permafrost is melting. The melting permafrost turns into something like mud, and the unstable ground can't support structures like roads or buildings that have been built on top of it. Melting permafrost is even worse for the world's climate, as it contributes to global warming (see page 144). In the Arctic, locked inside that frozen soil is more than 1.87 trillion tons (1.7 trillion t) of carbon dioxide. As the permafrost melts, this gas is released into the atmosphere, increasing global warming. The warming melts even more permafrost, which releases more gas, which raises the temperature ... and the cycle continues.

CAP IT OFF

The ice caps that make up the North and South Poles are so cold that very little wildlife can survive the extremes. It's so cold that even during the summer, the temperature rarely goes above freezing. In the Southern Hemisphere, Antarctica is the largest landmass with an ice cap climate. In the Northern Hemisphere, islands in the Arctic Ocean have this climate, along with parts of Greenland. The land in ice cap regions is permanently frozen, and plants cannot grow there.

Cold weather's for the birds!

PERMAFROST CAN BE DEEPER THAN 4,900 FEET (1,500 M).

Cool Facts About THE ARCTIC

The Arctic

NORTH AMERICA   EUROPE   ASIA
SOUTH AMERICA   AFRICA
AUSTRALIA
ANTARCTICA

Looking at a globe, one polar region seems to sit on top of the world: the Arctic. It's made up of all the land and sea within the Arctic Circle. The Arctic includes parts of eight nations: Canada, Denmark, Finland, Iceland, Norway, Sweden, Russia, and northern Alaska, U.S.A. Here are some cool facts about a cool place.

SNOWY OWLS HUNT BY HEARING THEIR PREY MOVING UNDERNEATH THE ICE.

>> THE SVALBARD GLOBAL SEED VAULT ON THE NORWEGIAN ISLAND OF SPITSBERGEN STORES FROZEN SEEDS FOR MORE THAN 6,000 KINDS OF CROPS. THE SEEDS CAN BE USED IF POLLUTION, PESTS, OR OTHER DANGERS WIPE OUT A SPECIES.

>> A LAYER OF BLUBBER UP TO TWO FEET (0.6 M) THICK HELPS BOWHEAD WHALES SURVIVE IN COLD ARCTIC WATERS.

THE CANADIAN POSTAL CODE FOR THE NORTH POLE IS HOH OHO— A REFERENCE TO SANTA CLAUS.

DURING MONTHS OF DARKNESS, SOME PEOPLE WEAR HEAD LAMPS AND THEY GO OUT IN PAIRS AND BRING A FLARE GUN, IN CASE THEY MEET A POLAR BEAR.

>>ABOUT FOUR MILLION PEOPLE LIVE IN THE ARCTIC, INCLUDING INDIGENOUS PEOPLE SUCH AS THE SÁMI, CHUKCHI, ALEUT, YUPIK, AND INUIT.

I feel nice and toasty!

A NARWHAL'S TUSK IS ACTUALLY A LONG TOOTH THAT GROWS THROUGH THE WHALE'S UPPER LIP.

SPECIAL HAIRS CALLED GUARD HAIRS HELP WARM POLAR BEARS. THESE HAIRS TRAP AIR, WHICH HELPS THE BEAR HOLD IN ITS BODY HEAT.

MORE FACTS ON THE NEXT SPREAD!

Cool Facts About
ANTARCTICA

NORTH AMERICA   EUROPE   ASIA
SOUTH AMERICA   AFRICA   AUSTRALIA
ANTARCTICA

You don't need to travel the globe to reach the windiest, driest, and coldest place on Earth. Only one destination can claim all of these climate superlatives: the continent of Antarctica. Unlike the Arctic, no Indigenous people live in this polar region. In fact, no one lives there all year round, though there are research bases that always have someone living at them. And no one country controls the continent. But about 30 countries do have research stations across Antarctica, where scientists and the people who help them work and live. Ready for some *brr*-illiant facts about the coldest continent?

>>WEDDELL SEALS CAN DIVE TO A DEPTH OF MORE THAN 2,300 FEET (720 M) IN THE WATERS OFF ANTARCTICA. THE SEALS' "BARKS" CAN BE HEARD ABOVE THE ICE.

CARGO SHIPS BRING MORE THAN 11 MILLION POUNDS (5,000 T) OF FOOD AND SUPPLIES TO THE RESEARCH BASE McMURDO STATION.

THE WARMEST TEMPERATURE EVER RECORDED AT THE SOUTH POLE WAS 9.9°F (-12.2°C).

>>LESS THAN ONE PERCENT OF ANTARCTICA IS NOT COVERED WITH ICE. IN SOME SPOTS THE ICE SHEET IS THREE MILES (4.8 KM) THICK.

Snow and wind don't slow me down!

IN 2022, ABOUT 4,000 PEOPLE APPLIED FOR THE FOUR JOB OPENINGS AT THE GOUDIER ISLAND POST OFFICE.

ABOUT FIVE MILLION PENGUINS CALL ANTARCTICA HOME.

>>THE MALE EMPEROR PENGUIN IS THE ONLY WARM-BLOODED ANIMAL THAT STAYS ON THE CONTINENT THROUGHOUT THE WINTER.

THE ADÉLIE PENGUIN BUILDS NESTS MADE OF ROCKS. AND ONE BIRD MIGHT EVEN STEAL SOME OF ITS NEIGHBOR'S ROCKS!

I'm not sure I fit in here!

SURVIVOR STORIES:
FIGHTING THE ICE

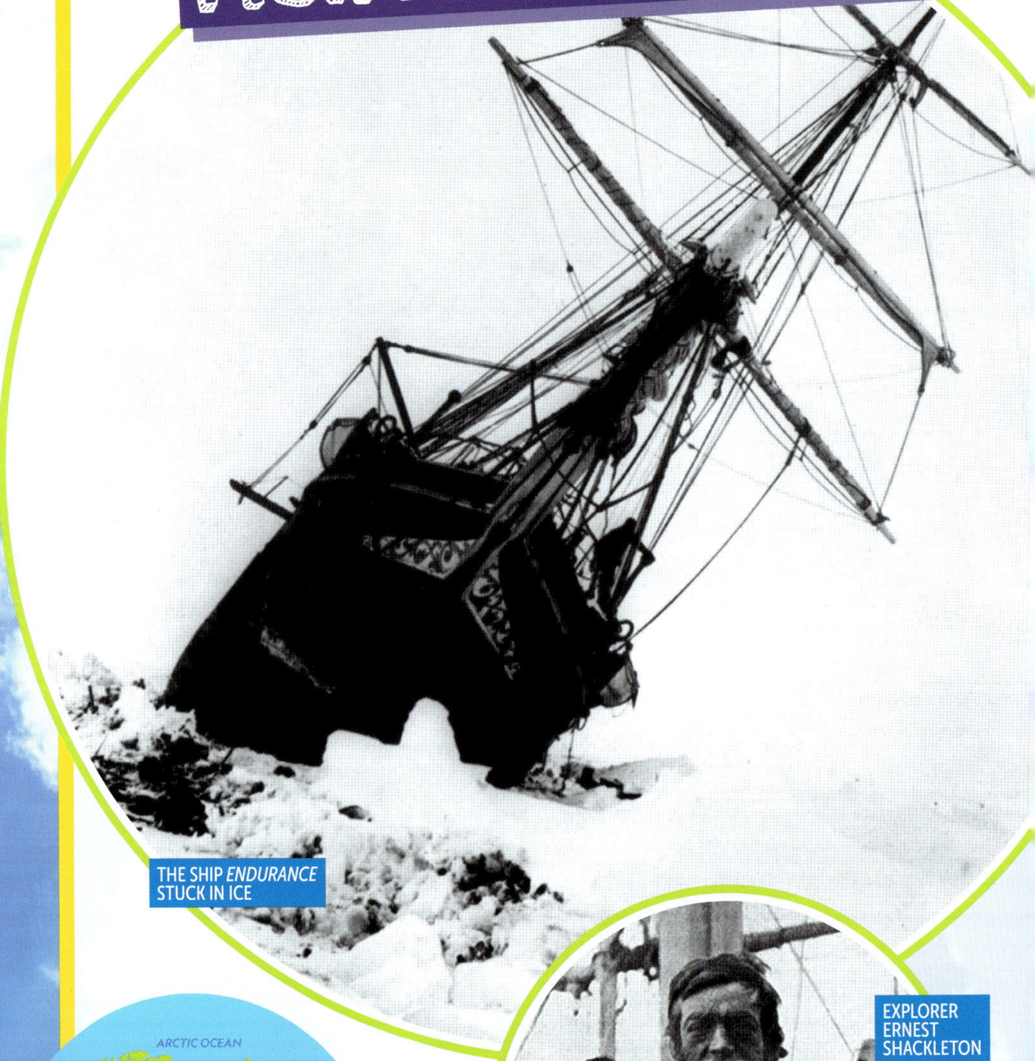

THE SHIP *ENDURANCE* STUCK IN ICE

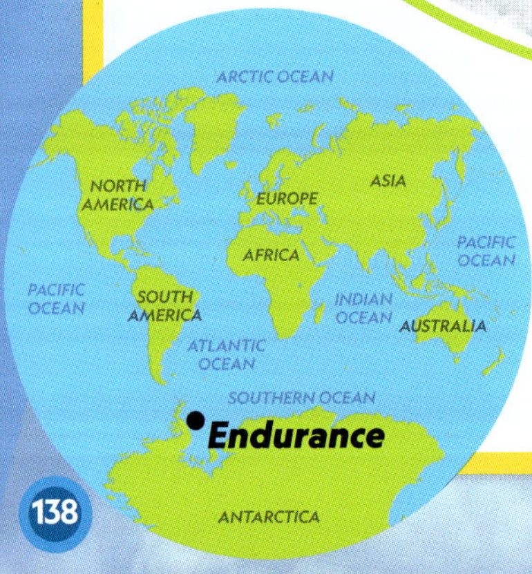

ARCTIC OCEAN
NORTH AMERICA
EUROPE
ASIA
PACIFIC OCEAN
AFRICA
PACIFIC OCEAN
SOUTH AMERICA
INDIAN OCEAN
AUSTRALIA
ATLANTIC OCEAN
SOUTHERN OCEAN
Endurance
ANTARCTICA

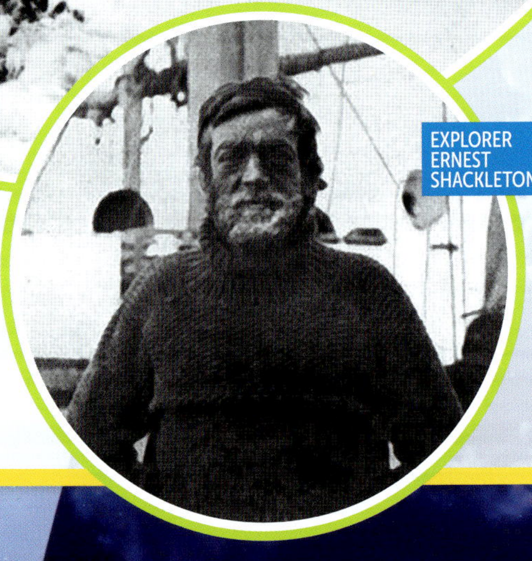

EXPLORER ERNEST SHACKLETON

British explorer Ernest Shackleton led expeditions to Antarctica twice. On his second voyage, in December 1914, he sailed from South Georgia Island. He and his crew of 27 were on a wooden ship called *Endurance*. The name seemed to indicate what was to come as Shackleton and the crew tried to endure, or survive, a terrible voyage.

STRANDED ON ICE

By January 1915, near the coast of Antarctica, *Endurance* became trapped in sea ice. The wind and ocean currents pushed the ice and the ship along. The crew could sometimes see land, but there was no way to reach it. In October, knowing the ice would crush the ship, Shackleton and his men abandoned *Endurance* and set up camp on an ice floe. Soon, they watched the mighty vessel sink into the ocean.

On their campsite of ice, the crew set up tents and hunted seals and penguins for food. In April 1916, the men saw openings in the ice, and they set off in small boats they had rescued from *Endurance*. After battling rough seas and cold winds, the crew finally reached solid land. Shackleton set up another camp, then took some of the healthiest crew members in one of the boats, hoping to find a ship that could rescue them.

LONG TRIP TO SAFETY

This new journey exposed Shackleton and his men to more terrible weather. The boat was just 23 feet (7 m) long, and a tidal wave almost sank it. At times, the men had to chip through heavy ice to keep moving. It took a little more than two weeks for the boat to reach South Georgia Island. Then the men had to reach one of the few settlements on the remote island. Shackleton and two other crew members walked over ice fields and mountains, a trek that took 36 hours. Finally, on May 20, 1916, they reached a whaling station.

Shackleton made arrangements for a larger ship to rescue the crew he had left behind. Icy waters and bad weather delayed the trip, but on August 30, a small steamer was finally able to reach them. Somehow, the entire crew of *Endurance* had survived more than 19 months trapped in polar ice.

ARCTIC SEA ICE

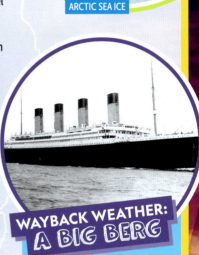

WAYBACK WEATHER: A BIG BERG

Ice from polar regions can drift for many miles, as the ocean liner *Titanic* discovered in 1912. An iceberg that formed in Greenland three years before was in the path of the gigantic ship, which was sailing from Ireland to New York on its first transatlantic voyage. When the iceberg first hit the water, it was 1,700 feet (518 m) long. Despite partially melting, it was still huge when the *Titanic* accidentally hit it on the night of April 14. After the impact, water flooded the ship and it sank, killing more than 1,500 people. Today, tools such as radar and GPS, along with planes sent to search the oceans, help ships avoid icebergs.

Weather Words

"A mild blizzard set in during the morning ... All day the wind screams in our rigging."

—*Endurance* photographer Frank Hurley, writing in his diary

In High PLACES

MOUNT KILIMANJARO, TANZANIA, AFRICA

TANZANIA'S MOUNT KILIMANJARO IS IN A TROPICAL REGION, BUT AT THE TOP, TEMPERATURES CAN FALL BELOW 0°F (-17.7°C).

In the years since Wladimir Köppen came up with his five climate types, other geographers have added more details to the system. During the 1960s, Glenn Trewartha of the United States suggested adding a sixth main climate category. He called it highlands, and it refers to the microclimate that can occur on mountains and plateaus.

Highlands climates can be found at any latitude, and they often have weather similar to the lower elevations around them. Because of that, there is no one standard highlands climate. But some things are generally true about the weather on and around mountains:

- The temperature goes down as you go up, with the mountain peak always cooler than its base. One example of this is Mount Kilimanjaro in Tanzania, near its border with Kenya.

- The side of a mountain that wind hits is called the windward side. As the wind moves up a mountain, it helps form clouds and precipitation. You read about an example of this on page 18. In general, the amount of precipitation increases at higher elevations.

- The opposite side of the mountain, called the leeward side, is usually drier and warmer.

- The time of day affects temperature, too. Eastern sides of mountains are warmed by the sun, but they cool down as the day goes on. The western side has the opposite—cool mornings and warmer afternoons.

PEAK PERFORMANCE

Some of the cities with the highest elevation are found in the Andes of South America. They include El Alto, Bolivia, which sits at more than 13,000 feet (4,000 m). As in other places, people and wildlife have adapted to the challenges of living in an extreme climate.

One challenge is breathing—the air at high elevations has less oxygen than air at sea level. People in the Andes have high levels of a protein called hemoglobin in their red blood cells. The increased hemoglobin carries more oxygen through the body. People of the Andes can breathe easily, while visitors to this region might huff and puff at the high elevations.

Like humans, one species of duck in the Andes has adapted over thousands of years. Its blood has high levels of hemoglobin and another protein that helps it use the oxygen that is available.

GREAT "GRAIN"

When people high in the Andes want a protein-packed meal, they often turn to quinoa. It's sometimes called a super grain, though it's actually a seed and not a grain. It's a relative of spinach. Quinoa is a great highlands crop, as it can be grown at elevations more than 12,000 feet (3,700 m). The rest of the world has also discovered this nutritious nugget, and new varieties grow in places far from the Andes, such as the tropical African nation of Rwanda.

EL ALTO, BOLIVIA, SOUTH AMERICA

A Changing CLIMATE

SMOKE FROM A PLANT BURNING COAL

Hot, cold, and everything in between—Earth has seen it. The climate in certain areas, or even worldwide, can change over many thousands of years. Sometimes the change occurs naturally, as when ice ages grip some or all of the planet. Earth has seen long warm periods, too. Small changes in Earth's orbit have played a part in these changes, as the planet receives less or more sunlight. But in recent years, scientists have seen that human activity is affecting Earth in a big and fast way.

WARMING WARNING

The average temperature on Earth has been warming rapidly since the Industrial Revolution. Starting around 1750, people began using machines that relied on fossil fuels to power them. Those fuels were first coal, then gasoline, and later, natural gas. Still used today, fossil fuels power engines, heat buildings, and generate electricity, among other uses.

Hold your breath!

During the 19th century, not many American women studied science, let alone became scientists. Eunice Newton Foote was an exception. In 1856, she conducted an experiment that helped shape our understanding of global warming. Foote filled several glass tubes with ordinary air, CO_2, and other gases, then put the tubes in sunlight. The tube with the CO_2 became hotter than the others and took longer to cool once Foote removed it from the sunlight. The tube got almost 20°F (11°C) hotter than the one with air. Foote concluded that CO_2 in the atmosphere could make Earth warmer.

Burning these fuels releases carbon dioxide (CO_2) and other gases into the atmosphere. During the 1950s, a U.S. scientist named Charles David Keeling and his colleagues perfected a way to measure how much CO_2 is in the air. He found 315 parts per million (ppm) of CO_2 in the air then. Over the next few decades, the number kept increasing, and by 2023 it was 420.8 ppm. That number keeps rising. The numbers are alarming because carbon dioxide in the air traps some heat that otherwise would rise into space.

Rising levels of carbon dioxide are one of the main reasons Earth's climate is getting warmer. The change isn't much each year—the world's average temperature has gone up just under 2°F (1°C) since 1880. But most of that increase has happened in the past 50 years. And the temperature is predicted to rise several more degrees by the end of this century, in part because of human fossil fuel use. Even these seemingly small changes in temperature can have severe effects across Earth.

SCIENTIST EUNICE NEWTON FOOTE

Too-Hot HOUSE

TRAFFIC IN LOS ANGELES, CALIFORNIA, U.S.A.

IF ALL CARBON DIOXIDE WAS REMOVED FROM EARTH'S ATMOSPHERE, THE GLOBAL TEMPERATURE WOULD PLUNGE BY ALMOST 59°F (33°C).

Carbon dioxide exists naturally in Earth's atmosphere. Some of it is released when you and other living creatures exhale. Other gases also enter the atmosphere from such things as volcanic eruptions or when dead plants rot in the sun. These gases include methane, nitrous oxide, and water vapor. Together, CO_2 and these other gases are called greenhouse gases.

A greenhouse is a building designed to keep plants warm so they can grow almost anywhere. Sunlight passes through glass panels and nourishes the plants. The plants then release some heat, which the glass holds inside the house, keeping everything toasty.

For Earth, the greenhouse gases are like those glass panels. The sun's energy passes through the gases. Then, the gases trap some of the heat that comes off of Earth's surface after it's warmed by the sun. Greenhouse gases are essential for keeping Earth warm enough to support life. But too much of the gases can have potentially disastrous effects.

HITTING THE GAS

As scientists have learned, you can have too much of a good thing. Human activity, such as burning fossil fuels, releases extra amounts of greenhouses gases into the atmosphere. That's what's causing the rising heat across Earth. Between 1990 and 2015, human activity caused the amount of greenhouse gases in the atmosphere to increase by 43 percent.

THE SUN'S ENERGY HITS EARTH'S SURFACE, THEN REFLECTS UPWARD INTO SPACE. MEANWHILE, SOME OF THE ENERGY GENERATED BY EARTH'S HEATED SURFACE IS TRAPPED CLOSE TO EARTH BY GREENHOUSE GASES.

METHANE MESS

CO_2 gets most of the blame for causing global warming, but methane plays a big part, too. It can trap more heat than CO_2 but it doesn't stay in the atmosphere nearly as long. Mining coal and drilling for natural gas and oil pump methane into the atmosphere—60 percent of it comes from human activity. Another big source of it? Cow burps! As cows digest their food, chemicals in their stomachs release methane, which the cows belch out. That's one reason some people are concerned about land being cleared to raise more cattle. Methane is also found in permafrost, and it's released as that frozen ground begins to melt (see page 133).

Excusez-moi!

WHERE DOES IT COME FROM?

In the United States, sources of greenhouse gases created by people include:

GASES	HUMAN ACTIVITY	PERCENTAGE OF ALL GREEN-HOUSE GASES
CO_2	BURNING FOSSIL FUELS, CUTTING DOWN FORESTS	79.4
METHANE	MINING COAL, DRILLING FOR NATURAL GAS AND OIL	11.5
NITROUS OXIDE	FARMING, BURNING FOSSIL FUELS	6.2
OTHER GASES	MAKING OF REFRIGERATION/ COOLING APPLIANCES AND SOME COMPUTER PARTS	3

Climate Change
CONSEQUENCES

You can't see greenhouse gases, but there's plenty of evidence of the effects of global warming. Here are some recent examples from the world around us.

RECORD HEAT

Earth is heating up—and fast. The hottest years ever recorded have occurred since 2014, and every decade since the 1980s has been warmer than the one before it. The rate of warming has been increasing in recent years, too, compared to just 50 years ago. The Arctic is warming nearly four times faster than the rest of the world. The region's warmest years since 1900 have all happened since 2010. Siberia, with its subarctic climate, saw its worst heat wave in 2023, with several cities setting new records as temperatures went over 100°F (38°C).

TAKING A SPIN

23,5°

Earth rotates once every 24 hours, making a day. It spins on its axis—an imaginary pole that goes through the planet's center. Over time, the position of the axis shifts slightly. Several years ago, scientists saw that the axis was moving a bit toward Canada. Then, it made a sharp turn to the east. This movement is caused in part by changes in where water is stored on and under Earth's surface. The melting of ice caps and glaciers, which is happening faster than ever because of global warming, plays a part in the axis's shift. So does the increased pumping of groundwater. Since 1993, more than two trillion tons (1.8 trillion t) of water have been pumped to the surface. The demand for that water could increase even more because global warming plays a part in how much precipitation may fall in a particular area (see page 153).

HEAVIER RAINS

Heavy rainstorms are more frequent in some parts of the world, and they can drop huge amounts of water. Climate change plays a part because it warms the oceans, which makes more water evaporate into the atmosphere, creating the conditions for more rain. In the future, that increased moisture is expected to also fuel more potent hurricanes and other tropical cyclones.

GLOBAL ACTION ON GLOBAL WARMING

In 1988, some people already saw the dangers of global warming. That led the United Nations and the World Meteorological Organization to create the Intergovernmental Panel on Climate Change (IPCC). Today, almost 200 nations are members of the IPCC. Its main job is to gather information on the effects of global warming and make predictions about its possible future effects. The IPCC also offers suggestions on how countries can reduce the damage caused by global warming.

BRINGING ON THE BLIZZARDS

Warming temperatures can also affect winter weather. The snowy season is getting shorter in some places, but extreme weather events like blizzards are packing a bigger punch. As the atmosphere warms, it can hold more moisture. When that moisture falls back to Earth as precipitation, and the temperatures are cold enough, a storm can dump lots of snow.

Ocean COMMOTION

BLEACHED CORALS IN THE MALDIVES, ASIA

IN 2023, WATERS OFF FLORIDA, U.S.A., REACHED **MORE THAN 100°F** (38°C)— AS WARM AS A **HOT TUB!**

Air temperatures are rising as a result of global warming. But the increased heat is affecting the world's oceans, too. Earth's oceans absorb almost all the extra heat produced by humans burning fossil fuels.

IN HOT WATER

Just as extreme heat waves can make the land hot, they can also do the same to the oceans. In 2023, ocean waters off the United Kingdom and parts of Europe experienced what meteorologists called an extreme marine heat wave, while in some areas the warmth was "beyond extreme." The temperature of the water surface was 9°F (5°C) higher than normal, the highest temperature in more than 170 years.

Later in 2023, the world's oceans saw the warmest temperatures ever recorded from January to September in any one year. Computer programs estimated that global warming played a part in the marine heat wave. Extreme marine heat waves can make it harder for marine wildlife to have babies or find food. In some cases, the heat waves kill the animals.

CURRENT EVENTS

Warming waters can also affect ocean currents that play a part in shaping climates. The Atlantic Ocean is home to a system of currents called the Atlantic Meridional Overturning Circulation (AMOC). The AMOC carries warm water to the northern part of the Atlantic and brings cold water down south. It's part of a worldwide system of "conveyor belts" that move around warm and cold water. Because of global warming, the odds are increasing that the AMOC could be disrupted. What would happen?

Scientists already know that the AMOC's speed has slowed over the past century. Some of this occurs as a result of natural changes in the climate, but some experts fear the AMOC could slow down even more as global temperatures keep rising. That could affect the Gulf Stream, which shapes weather in parts of northern Europe. That current has already brought warmer waters to parts of the East Coast of the United States, prompting some fish to move farther north to find the cooler waters they like. That makes it harder for fishers to catch fish for food.

A weaker AMOC could cause ocean temperatures in the North Atlantic to rise even more. Other ocean waters would cool, making the air in the atmosphere cooler, so temperatures would fall. Rain levels would increase south of the Equator but decrease in other areas. That change would affect farming, and perhaps lead to rising food costs.

ATLANTIC MERIDIONAL OVERTURNING CIRCULATION

A MARINE BUOY WITH SOLAR PANELS

Polar PROBLEMS

I think I may be underdressed!

MELTING ICEBERGS IN ANTARCTICA

Weather Words

"Each year we're losing an area [of Arctic sea ice] that's roughly the size of West Virginia."

—sea ice scientist Rachel Tilling, Ph.D.

WEST VIRGINIA

arth's polar regions can be hostile places for people and wildlife. But they play an important role in the planet's climate. Polar climates help create sea ice, which is ice that forms in the water. This ice covers about 15 percent of Earth's oceans during at least part of the year, and in the coldest spots, the ice never melts. Sea ice helps reflect some of the sun's heat back into the atmosphere and prevents heat from the water from entering the atmosphere.

Sea ice also plays a role in the global conveyor belt of ocean currents. As the ice forms, it pushes cold, salty water below the surface. That water is carried southward by the AMOC and other currents.

SLIPPING AWAY

Global warming is having a bad impact on the polar regions, particularly in the Arctic. Sea ice there keeps decreasing every year. Storms in the region are part of the

MAP KEY

■ Minimum sea ice extent

problem, as strong winds and storm surges melt some of the ice. As in other regions, storms like these are expected to get stronger with global warming. Warming sea and air temperatures also melt Arctic ice, and that will keep increasing, because of a cycle—less sea ice means less heat from the sun is reflected back into the atmosphere. The exposed water absorbs the heat. And the oceans lose the ice "blanket" that keeps their heat out of the atmosphere. All the existing sea ice that currently remains through the Arctic summer could be gone by 2035.

Other forms of polar ice are melting, too. When sea ice melts, it doesn't add more water to the oceans—it just goes from a solid to a liquid. But glaciers and other types of ice that form on land are a different story. When they melt, they add water to the oceans. Sea levels around the world have gone up a little over eight inches (20 cm) in the last century. The rising sea levels cause flooding and can even force whole towns to move farther inland, away from the coast (see page 159).

Melting glaciers can also add to global warming. In parts of Arctic Norway, the melting glaciers expose land that had been covered for years. Groundwater bubbles up from beneath the land and forms small ponds. The water contains the greenhouse gas methane. The gas comes from the decayed remains of ancient plants and animals, and scientists think there could be a lot of it. As with melting sea ice, the melting glaciers in Norway could create a loop that only makes global warming worse.

LIFE ON THE ICE

In the Arctic, sea ice is home to foxes, polar bears, and seals. In Antarctica, penguins live on the floating floes. And underneath the ice, the salty water is home to tiny sea creatures that become food for larger polar animals.

Warming WOES

EXTREME HEAT
SAVE POWER 4–9PM
STAY COOL

A fire in wintertime can keep us cozy and warm. And a hot drink warms us up on a cold day. But global warming can be a dangerous type of heat—for the whole planet. Here's a deeper dive into how global warming will present challenges to people in the decades ahead.

RISING TEMPS

Temperatures have been on the rise over the past 50 years, and that's expected to continue if human activity impacting global warming keeps going at the same pace. Already, heat waves wash over the United States more often, and for longer periods, than they did 60 years ago. The extreme heat affects everyone, but especially the elderly and people who are sick. Around the world, between 1998 and 2017, more than 166,000 people died from extreme heat. That number could keep climbing.

You're my biggest fan!

Did You Know?

Extreme heat is deadlier in the U.S. than tornadoes, hurricanes, and floods combined.

RISING SEA LEVELS

Sea levels are on the rise, too, and for two major reasons: Ice on land is melting, sending water into the seas, and warmer temperatures make ocean water expand. The rate of increase has almost doubled since 1993. That means low-lying cities might have more frequent floods. By 2040, Miami, Florida, U.S.A., is expecting to see sea levels rise at least 10 inches (25 cm) compared with the levels in 2000. Places in the city that once flooded only a few times a year now see up to a dozen floods. And people in Miami aren't the only ones who need to think about rising seas. About 40 percent of Americans live in coastal communities. Worldwide, more than two billion people live in coastal areas—that's about 25 percent of everyone on Earth. Flooding could also increase because some areas will see more rainfall. Warming temperatures mean more evaporation of water in rivers, lakes, and other bodies of water. That adds more moisture to the water cycle.

WATER SHORTAGES

While global change will bring more water to coastal cities, other parts of the world will find it harder to get hydrated. Already, several billion people each year struggle to get enough water for all their needs. Global warming adds to the problem. In many parts of the world, melting snow provides water for drinking and raising crops. Higher temperatures during the winter mean less snow, and what does hit the ground can melt too quickly for farmers to use during the summer. Glaciers are an important source of fresh water, too, and they're quickly disappearing (see page 150). Water resources also dry up during extended droughts, which are on the rise. And droughts bring an increased risk for wildfires.

DISCOVER MORE ON NEXT SPREAD!

Warming WOES
CONTINUED

UNPREDICTABLE WEATHER

Rain is good for farmers, but global warming could result in unpredictable weather and too much or too little precipitation. Heat waves and droughts can dry up farmland and kill crops and livestock. Floods can damage crops or make it impossible to harvest them when they're ripe. Too much rain can also hurt plants. Global warming is also extending the growing season in some regions. Farmers may be able to plant and harvest more in one year, but they might need to spend more money on irrigating the crops to fight the effects of heat waves. And more water for crops could mean less water for drinking and other uses.

Warming temperatures also affect bees and other insects. Farmers rely on them to pollinate many of their crops—a process that creates a plant's seeds. Pollinators need the pollen that flowers produce, but changes in temperature mean the flowers might not bloom.

Bee-lieve me, this is busy work!

BYE-BYE FRIES?

Say it isn't so! Global warming could affect the beloved french fry. Americans wolf down an average of 34 pounds (15 kg) of fries per person every year. The potatoes used to make those fries enjoy cooler climates, such as those found in the leading potato-growing U.S. states: Washington, Idaho, and Wisconsin. As temperatures go up, the levels of sugar in the spud are affected, too, which leads to french fries that are too brown. More heat also makes it harder for potatoes to fight off diseases that harm the plant.

INCREASED ILLNESS

Longer and stronger heat waves are affecting human health, but the heat harms us in other ways, too. A warmer atmosphere creates the conditions that can increase harmful air pollution. The dirty air can be particularly bad for people with lung diseases. Floods can release harmful bacteria into the water. People who walk through flooded streets or get trapped in flooded homes can get sick from the bacteria. Warmer, wetter weather in some places also means more mosquitoes. These biting pests carry diseases that can be deadly. The insects are also moving into areas where they've never lived, as global warming has created conditions that they like. This then brings mosquito-borne illnesses to places where they didn't exist before.

Facing
TROUBLED TIMES

A round the world, some spots are already feeling the effects of a warming climate. Here are just a few examples.

Arctic

NORTH AMERICA
Glacier National Park

EUROPE
Mount Everest

ASIA

Japan

AFRICA

Maldives

SOUTH AMERICA
Amazon Rainforest

AUSTRALIA

ANTARCTICA

GLACIER NATIONAL PARK, MONTANA, U.S.A.

What's a national park named for its glaciers going to do when the glaciers are gone? People may soon find out. When the park was founded in 1910, it had 150 of the slow-moving ice "rivers." Now the park has fewer than 30 glaciers. And the ones still there are melting at a rapid rate, in part because the park is warming twice as fast as the rest of the world.

THE ARCTIC

You've read about the effects of global warming in the Arctic (see page 150). The heat has brought a major change to the region—ships can now sometimes sail through the sea ice during summer months. This "Northwest Passage" creates a shorter route between the Atlantic and Pacific Oceans. But ships making the voyage face the risk of sailing through more fog, formed by the melting ice. That increases the chances of an accident, which could lead to oil or chemical spills.

JAPAN

Tourists flock to Japan every spring to see the beautiful pink and white blossoms on the nation's cherry trees. Thanks to global warming, the trees are starting to bloom up to 11 days earlier than usual. That change could affect the timing of festivals that celebrate the flowers, which are a symbol of Japan. Blossom gazing is a big business, as people from around the world come to see the trees. The change in the flowering date could disrupt some of the celebrations. And warmer winters could one day keep the trees from blossoming at all.

THE AMAZON RAINFOREST, SOUTH AMERICA

The Amazon is home to more than three million species of wildlife. Global warming is making parts of the tropical rainforest hotter and drier—more like the climate found in a savanna. Massive cutting of trees is also affecting their habitat. For mammals in particular, these changes present challenges because many prefer to live in the forest rather than in a savanna environment. These animals include big cats, such as jaguars and ocelots, anteaters, and some deer.

THE MALDIVES, INDIAN OCEAN

This country is made up of almost 1,200 coral islands. Most of them are only about three feet (0.9 m) above sea level. Rising seawater presents a huge problem to these low-lying islands. By one estimate, people will not be able to live on some of the lowest islands by 2050. The government is trying one solution to help the residents who remain by building new islands with higher elevations. Sand is pumped from the ocean floor and spread over a coral platform. More than 50,000 people already live on one of these new islands, and its population could reach 200,000.

MOUNT EVEREST, NEPAL/CHINA BORDER

At 29,032 feet (8,849 m), the top of this mountain is the highest spot on Earth. And the Sherpa, the Indigenous people who live around it, are seeing how global warming is affecting this prized peak. Temperatures there are rising faster than the global average, leading to glacier erasure. It's taken just 30 years to melt the amount of glacial ice that forms over 2,000 years. That massive melt means in the future, people all over South Asia will have less drinking water.

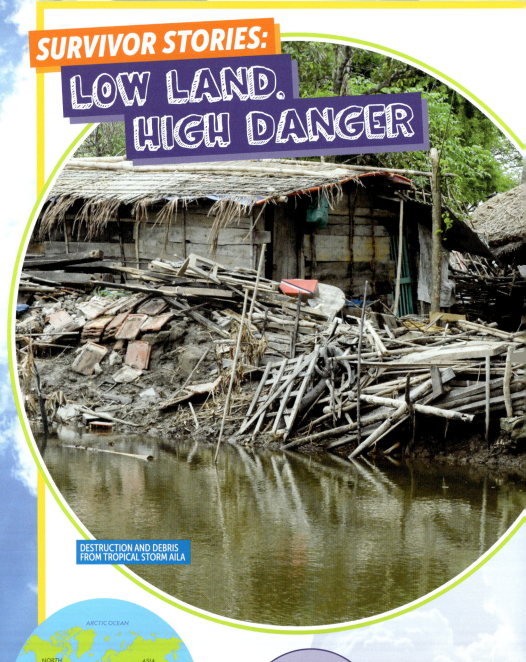

SURVIVOR STORIES:
LOW LAND, HIGH DANGER

DESTRUCTION AND DEBRIS FROM TROPICAL STORM AILA

ARCTIC OCEAN

NORTH AMERICA

EUROPE

ASIA

ATLANTIC OCEAN

Aila, India and Bangladesh

PACIFIC OCEAN

PACIFIC OCEAN

SOUTH AMERICA

AFRICA

INDIAN OCEAN

AUSTRALIA

SOUTHERN OCEAN

ANTARCTICA

Did You Know?

Worldwide, there will be an estimated 216 million internal climate migrants by 2050.

On May 25, 2009, tropical storm Aila hit eastern India and the neighboring country of Bangladesh. By cyclone standards, it wasn't an extremely powerful storm—its winds peaked at just 75 miles an hour (120 km/h) before it came ashore. But the region that Aila struck is barely above sea level, and the storm surge and rain proved deadly. More than 250 people died because of the storm, and an estimated one million people were left homeless.

SURGE SURVIVOR

In Bangladesh, the storm surge was particularly destructive. The entire island of Nijhum Dwip was reportedly covered in water, and across the country, at least 500,000 people had to leave their homes because of floods. One of them was Musamat Meherunesa from the village of Gabura. She and her family had survived another cyclone, Sidr, that struck just 18 months before. After Aila, she came home to find her house destroyed. From then on, her family kept all their belongings in plastic containers, wondering when the next flood might come.

ON THE MOVE

Many storm survivors in Bangladesh became internal climate migrants. They move within the country to towns and cities away from the coast, hoping to escape the next flood. Bangladesh is increasingly feeling the effects of climate change. The rise of sea levels and the threat of stronger storms puts millions of people at risk. It's thought that by 2050, Bangladesh could lose about 17 percent of its land because it will be covered with water. That same year, the country could have almost 20 million internal migrants, forced to move because of the threats of global warming.

SALTY SOIL

The floods and rising sea levels in Bangladesh force some people to move because they can no longer grow their own food. Salty seawater often covers many fields. Once the water evaporates, the salt remains, and many crops won't grow in the salty soil. But in recent years, there has been some hope for Bangladeshi farmers near the coast. They're planting seeds for crops that do grow in the salty ground, including carrots, beets, and potatoes.

TROPICAL STORM AILA CAUSED TREMENDOUS DAMAGE.

FLOOD FEARS

Bangladeshis can face floods even when no cyclone hits. Heavy rains during monsoon season can raise water levels in the country's rivers. That was the case in 2022, when extreme rains in June caused the worst flooding in more than a century. The floods almost completely covered two towns and left a total of 7.2 million people homeless. They also destroyed crops worth $12.5 million. The government of Bangladesh spends several billion dollars each year to try to prepare for the effects of global warming on the country. But one study suggested that if global temperatures keep rising, the risk of flooding will increase.

Wildlife WOES

The harmful changes global warming is bringing not only threaten people but plants, animals, and other living things, too. It's estimated that half of the species in some environments, including the Amazon, parts of Australia, and parts of Africa, could become extinct by 2100. Even if temperatures don't rise as high as some estimates say they could, thousands of species are at risk of disappearing. And global warming could be the last straw for animals already close to extinction.

What makes experts worry about wildlife? Rising temperatures and more frequent droughts can destroy a species' habitat—the area it calls its home. Habitat destruction can force animals to migrate to new areas to find food, which can make their life harder or even be deadly. Wildlife can also be forced out of their habitat or killed by natural disasters fueled by rising temperatures.

Over the next few pages, you'll read about just some of the animals at high risk because of global warming.

Did You Know?

In 2019–2020, billions of animals in Australia were forced to flee or were killed in wildfires.

These paws weren't made for so much walking!

CORALS

Corals are tiny colorful sea creatures that form shells. Over time, millions of the corals form a coral reef, which becomes a home for other sea life. Fish and other organisms come to find food and shelter and raise their young. But tropical coral reefs are threatened by both warming waters and higher levels of acid in the ocean, which is caused by more carbon dioxide in the atmosphere. Rising temperatures kill the even smaller sea creatures called algae that the corals use as food. The algae also give the corals their color. As the algae die, the corals and the reefs they form turn white. This process is called bleaching, and a white reef is a sick one. When extreme bleaching occurs, the corals are at risk of dying. If they die, the sea life that rely on them could be harmed, too.

POLAR BEARS

The Arctic's most famous animal faces a serious sea ice challenge. The sea ice is a floating platform that polar bears use to hunt for seals, to mate, or to take a much needed rest after hours of swimming. As the ice melts, the bears have to swim farther to find hunting grounds, and they can drown as they search. They're also forced to spend more time on land, where they struggle to find food. Some days, they can't find any food at all. In part of Alaska in 2020, bears went more than 130 days without eating.

Did You Know?

About 25 percent of all fish in the oceans depend on coral reefs to survive.

DISCOVER MORE ON NEXT SPREAD!

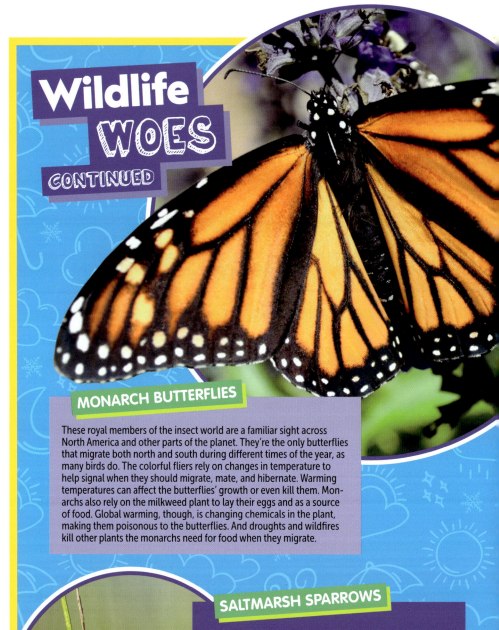

Wildlife WOES
CONTINUED

MONARCH BUTTERFLIES

These royal members of the insect world are a familiar sight across North America and other parts of the planet. They're the only butterflies that migrate both north and south during different times of the year, as many birds do. The colorful fliers rely on changes in temperature to help signal when they should migrate, mate, and hibernate. Warming temperatures can affect the butterflies' growth or even kill them. Monarchs also rely on the milkweed plant to lay their eggs and as a source of food. Global warming, though, is changing chemicals in the plant, making them poisonous to the butterflies. And droughts and wildfires kill other plants the monarchs need for food when they migrate.

SALTMARSH SPARROWS

This tiny bird is found only along the coasts of the eastern United States. It builds its nest in the grass found near marshes. Until now, the birds knew where to build nests so they could avoid the water from high tides and storms. But rising sea levels pose a threat to their nests and the eggs inside them. The waters can flood the nests. If the birds build the nests farther away from the water, they increase the odds of becoming a predator's snack. These dangers, along with the loss of habitat when people build near the shore, has raised the risk of saltmarsh sparrows becoming extinct.

MOTHER SEA TURTLES ALONG PART OF THE AUSTRALIAN COAST **HAVE LAID EGGS** THAT **PRODUCED ALMOST ALL FEMALES.**

SEA TURTLES

Sea turtles lay their eggs in sandy beaches. The temperature of the sand influences whether the baby turtle that hatches is a male or female. When the sand goes above about 89°F (31.6°C), a mother has fewer male than female babies. With fewer males, the species has a more difficult time reproducing. Global warming, with rising sea levels and more rain, can also destroy the beaches where turtles lay their eggs.

INTRUDER ALERT!

Global warming can also increase the threat of invasive species, animals that were taken from their natural habitat and introduced into a new one. Sometimes humans make this move on purpose, but other times it happens by accident—a species ends up on a ship and is carried far from home. In their new habitat, the invasive species might harm existing wildlife. In Australia, the cane toad is an invasive species. This amphibian can weigh up to three pounds (1.4 kg). Its skin is highly poisonous, and the toad has been known to dine on small mammals and to poison pets that pick them up in their mouths. The toads have also nearly wiped out one wild animal native to Australia, the northern quoll, a distant relative of kangaroos. Global warming is no sweat for the toads, as their bodies easily adapt to the heat, compared to other cold-blooded critters. Other invasive species that can tolerate or even thrive in warm and wet environments are poised to spread if the planet continues to warm.

I'm *TOAD*-ally in trouble!

Fears for the RAINFOREST

A STREAM IN A TEMPERATE RAINFOREST

MOISTURE CREATED BY PLANT TRANSPIRATION IN THE AMAZON CAN FALL AS RAIN AS FAR AWAY AS TEXAS, WHICH IS MORE THAN 2,000 MILES (3,200 KM) AWAY.

Global warming is bringing changes to the world's tropical rainforests, which are areas that receive at least 70 inches (178 cm) of rainfall per year. The impact of these changes spreads beyond the rainforests because they play a helpful role throughout the global environment. Both tropical rainforests and temperate rainforests, usually found in coastal, mountainous areas like North America's Pacific Northwest, are affected by rising temperatures.

A NATURAL HELPER

Rainforests are home to an incredible number of wildlife species, as well as millions of people. The plants in the forest are an important part of the water cycle, which spreads precipitation all over the world. As the plants take energy from the sun, they transpire, or release water in the form of vapor. Some of that water remains in the rainforest, but some of it evaporates and spreads to other regions in clouds.

MAP KEY

- Temperate rainforest
- Tropical rainforest

Rainforests also remove carbon dioxide (CO_2), a greenhouse gas, from the atmosphere. The plants use CO_2 to help convert the sun's energy into the sugar they use as food, a process called photosynthesis. Along with creating food, photosynthesis releases oxygen into the air. Almost all of the planet's oxygen comes from plants and tiny sea creatures that also use photosynthesis to live.

HARMFUL HEATING

How does global warming hurt rainforests? Higher temperatures mean some areas are getting less rain and may even experience droughts. For rainforests everywhere, that raises the risk of forest fires, which kill the forest and release the carbon dioxide stored in the plants. More CO_2 adds to the global warming problem. In temperate climates, droughts can also mean species that thrive in humidity and moisture will struggle to survive.

Droughts and wildfires in the forests could also fuel a vicious cycle. Fewer trees and other plants would mean less water is available through transpiration to add to the water cycle. Fewer clouds will form, meaning less rain would fall, which would increase the risk of more droughts.

FIRES IN THE AMAZON RAINFOREST

A STEP BACKWARD

The Amazon, the world's largest tropical rainforest, has always played a key role in absorbing carbon dioxide. It takes in about 25 percent of all the CO_2 absorbed by land across the planet. But in 2021, scientists noticed a major shift. Part of the Amazon was beginning to release more of the greenhouse gas than it absorbed. This was caused in part by fires, many of which were set by people to clear land for farming. But some of the CO_2 also came from wildfires. And warmer, drier conditions make it harder for trees and other plants to store CO_2. Because of these conditions in the Amazon, scientists think it is losing its position as one of the world's best absorbers of CO_2. The tropical rainforest in the Democratic Republic of the Congo will likely become the most important absorber of CO_2.

AN AERIAL VIEW OF TREES BURNING IN BRAZIL

Seeking SOLUTIONS

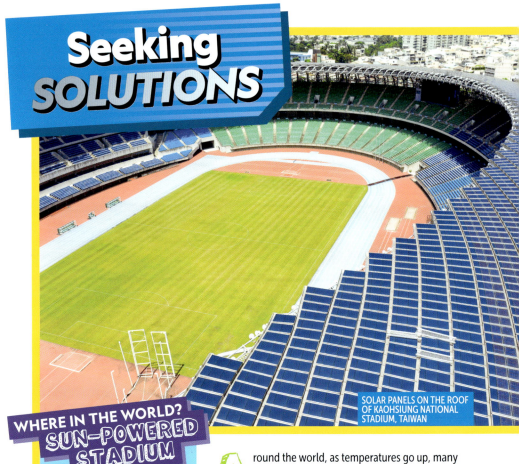

SOLAR PANELS ON THE ROOF OF KAOHSIUNG NATIONAL STADIUM, TAIWAN

WHERE IN THE WORLD?
SUN-POWERED STADIUM

On the Asian island of Taiwan, 55,000 people can fill Kaohsiung National Stadium, but they don't have to worry about how much CO_2 the giant arena produces. That's because Kaohsiung is the world's largest solar-powered stadium. The stadium is in the shape of a giant snake or dragon. What looks like the beast's scales are actually the panels that soak up the sun's rays. When the stadium is quiet, the power it generates can be fed into the local electricity network.

EUROPE ASIA
NORTH AMERICA
Kaohsiung National Stadium•
SOUTH AMERICA AFRICA AUSTRALIA
ANTARCTICA

Around the world, as temperatures go up, many people are taking action. Here are some of the ways people are trying to reduce the amount of greenhouse gas in the atmosphere created by human activity.

RENEWABLE ENERGY

From solar panels on homes to giant wind farms, people are turning away from fossil fuels to generate electricity. Instead, they use power from the wind, sun, water, and heat created deep underground. All of these are sources of renewable energy, meaning they won't run out. And they don't produce CO_2. Renewable energy will soon become the world's largest source of electrical power.

ELECTRIC VEHICLES

More cars and trucks that run on rechargeable batteries are rolling out of factories and hitting the road. Not only do they not produce greenhouse gases, they're also easier to maintain than vehicles

AN ELECTRIC CAR CHARGES.

that run on gasoline or diesel fuel. Several companies have begun producing the first electric planes.

CARBON CAPTURE

Along with trying to produce less CO_2, some companies are trying to suck up the gas before it even enters the atmosphere. Carbon-capture technology aims to collect CO_2 at the places where fossil fuels are burned to generate electricity or at factories that produce a lot of it. The captured gas is then stored deep underground. These projects store about 45 million tons (40.8 million t) of CO_2 every year—about the same amount produced by 10 million cars. Another capture project features concrete that pulls CO_2 from air as the concrete hardens. Another benefit? The gas actually makes the concrete stronger.

THIS COAL-FIRED POWER STATION HAS CARBON CAPTURE CAPABILITIES.

Almost 50 years ago, Veerabhadran Ramanathan saw that carbon dioxide was not the only gas warming the planet. A professor of atmospheric science, Ramanathan realized that a group of gases called halocarbons were also a danger. These gases occur naturally, but some were produced by air conditioners and refrigerators, too. Ramanathan also saw that reducing the amount of those gases in the atmosphere was a big step in fighting global warming. His work helped shape an international agreement called the Montreal Protocol. Its goal is to eliminate gases that were depleting ozone, a gas above Earth that screens out some of the sun's harmful forms of energy. Those gases also add to global warming. A later addition to the Montreal Protocol slowed the use of other, related greenhouse gases.

BY THE NUMBERS

World Leaders in Renewable Energy

PERCENTAGE OF ELECTRICAL POWER THAT COMES FROM RENEWABLE ENERGY (2022)	
NORWAY	98.5
BRAZIL	89.2
NEW ZEALAND	86.6
COLOMBIA	75.1
CANADA	68.8

Explorers in
THE FIELD

National Geographic supports Explorers—individuals around the world who study a range of topics. Some Explorers focus on the effects of global warming and try to find ways to fight it. Here's a look at three of them.

NORTH AMERICA
EUROPE
ASIA
AFRICA
SOUTH AMERICA
AUSTRALIA
ANTARCTICA
SOUTHERN OCEAN

Ana-Belén Yánez Suárez

Tabe Brandon Njume

Jane Younger

JANE YOUNGER

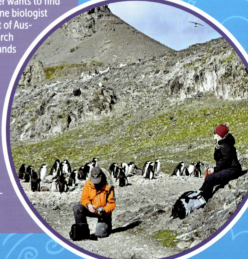

How are penguins in and around the Antarctic doing as the region warms? Jane Younger wants to find out. Younger is a marine biologist based in Tasmania, part of Australia. She has done research on Antarctica and nearby islands to see how a changing polar climate is affecting the birds, along with mammals that live in the Southern Ocean. One concern is that the warming might make penguins more likely to catch certain diseases. On one research trip to the region, Younger and her team used a drone to count several species of penguins. Their research also took a stinky turn as the team collected penguin poop! The waste tells Younger and other researchers what the birds are eating and how that changes as the temperature rises.

KRILL CRISIS

Krill are tiny crustaceans that are a food source for many marine animals, including penguins. Some of these animals rely on krill for almost their entire diet. Krill populations have decreased because of warming waters. Rising levels of carbon dioxide also increase the amount of acid in the water, which further threatens the krill. A decline in the number of krill will make life harder for penguins.

TABE BRANDON NJUME

Mangrove forests are found along coasts in tropical and subtropical climates. Like other plants, they help remove carbon dioxide from the atmosphere, which is why Tabe Brandon Njume knows it's important to keep them healthy. But in his homeland of Cameroon, in Central Africa, people often cut down the mangrove trees for firewood and charcoal. As a college student, Njume helped start Greensphere Cameroon. The organization takes food waste and turns it into a kind of charcoal that people can burn instead of mangrove wood. The charcoal helps save the trees and reduces the amount of food waste thrown away. It's also cheaper than wood-based charcoal and doesn't produce the black, smelly smoke that comes from burning the mangrove charcoal.

ANA-BELÉN YÁNEZ SUÁREZ

Rising ocean temperatures is one of the many effects of climate change. These warming waters lead to areas with low oxygen, which affects the health of the animals living there. Ana-Belén Yánez Suárez, a marine biologist from Ecuador, is dedicated to helping protect deep-sea corals in the Galápagos and Isla del Coco. Her early work focused on how global warming affects tropical corals, but now she studies those living more than 650 feet (200 m) deep in cold waters. Suárez is researching how these deep-sea corals are distributed in low-oxygen areas and hopes to protect these fragile ecosystems as well as the species— like octopuses and cat sharks—that depend on them for food.

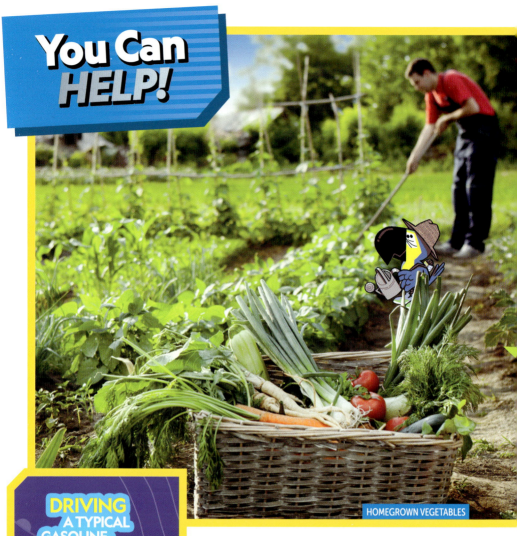

HOMEGROWN VEGETABLES

DRIVING A TYPICAL GASOLINE-POWERED CAR FOR JUST ONE MILE (1.6 KM) RELEASES ALMOST ONE POUND (.45 KG) OF CARBON DIOXIDE.

You may have heard of a "carbon footprint." No one is walking around with shoes made of carbon. The term refers to the amount of carbon dioxide and other greenhouse gases people use as they go about their lives. From turning on a light switch to flying in a plane, all sorts of actions create these harmful gases. But there are actions you, your friends, and your family can do to shrink your carbon footprint.

TURN IT OFF

For most Americans, what adds the most to their carbon footprint is what they do at home. You don't directly produce greenhouse gases when you turn on a computer or turn up the thermostat. But the power plants that create electricity often use fossil fuels. Some ways to reduce your carbon footprint at home include:

➤ Turning off lights and appliances when you're not using them. And some appliances, such as TVs and printers, continue to draw energy as long as they're plugged in. Try to unplug as many devices as you can when you're not using them. Use power strips so you can easily turn off several things at once.

➤ Turning up the AC, turning down the furnace: Ideally, air conditioners should run at 78°F (25.5°C) to keep you cool and save energy. In winter, the sweet spot for your furnace is 68°F (20°C) during the day, and a little cooler at night.

DRIVE LESS

For most Americans, transportation makes up a lot of their carbon footprint. Some ways to reduce greenhouse gases when on the move include:

- avoiding drive-through windows at restaurants and other businesses;
- using public transportation when it's available;
- combining all your family errands into one trip; and
- walking or riding a bicycle.

MAKE MENU CHANGES

When dinnertime comes, consider this: Growing and transporting food is a major source of greenhouse gases in the United States. Raising animals for meat, eggs, and dairy and then getting them to stores creates more than 75 percent of a food item's carbon footprint. Some ways to cut down on the greenhouse gases and still stay full include:

- eating meat with a smaller carbon footprint— chicken is better than beef;
- eating less meat, seafood, dairy, and eggs; and
- growing your own fruits and vegetables, or eating locally grown foods when you can.

Who you calling a chicken?

PLANTING AHEAD

If your family plants a tree today, it can help reduce your carbon footprint tomorrow. An adult tree can absorb 48 pounds (22 kg) of carbon dioxide each year!

Meteorological MARVELS

>>A METEOROLOGIST IN ARKANSAS WAS ABLE TO BAKE CINNAMON ROLLS AND COOKIES INSIDE A HOT CAR!

ONE DERECHO, A POWERFUL KIND OF WINDSTORM, HIT WISCONSIN IN 1998 WITH WINDS OF ALMOST 130 MILES AN HOUR (209 KM/H).

SPRITES, PIXIES, AND ELVES ARE LIGHTS THAT SOMETIMES APPEAR JUST ABOVE THUNDERSTORMS. THEY LAST FOR JUST A TINY FRACTION OF A SECOND AND CAN EXTEND FOR MANY MILES.

>> DURING A THUNDERSTORM, BRIGHTLY COLORED ELECTRICAL CHARGES CALLED ST. ELMO'S FIRE SOMETIMES SHOOT FROM POINTY OBJECTS, LIKE THE TOP OF CELL PHONE TOWERS OR THE TIPS OF AIRPLANE WINGS.

THE 30-30-30 RULE: WHEN THE TEMPERATURE HITS **-30°F** (-34°C) AND THE WIND IS **30 MILES AN HOUR** (48 KM/H), EXPOSED SKIN CAN FREEZE IN JUST **30 SECONDS.**

>>A KIND OF PRECIPITATION CALLED GRAUPEL FORMS WHEN WATER DROPLETS WITH A TEMPERATURE BELOW FREEZING ATTACH TO A SNOW CRYSTAL.

A "FIRENADO" HAPPENS WHEN SPINNING WINDS FORM ABOVE A WILDFIRE, CARRYING HOT AIR, ASH, AND BURNING EMBERS INTO THE SKY.

TO SURVIVE IN A HOT DESERT CLIMATE, A SAGUARO CACTUS CAN STORE OVER **1,000 GALLONS** (3,785 L) OF WATER IN ITS PRICKLY BODY AND LIMBS. **IT CAN GO A YEAR** WITHOUT STORING MORE.

>> AT SEA, SOME HURRICANES CREATE LARGE WAVES THAT ROLL DOWN TO THE OCEAN FLOOR, CAUSING VIBRATIONS CALLED "STORMQUAKES."

Build Your Own
WEATHER STATION

You can play meteorologist at home by making your own weather station. A basic station would have the following items:

- a thermometer to measure temperature
- a barometer to measure air pressure
- a hygrometer to measure humidity
- an anemometer to measure wind speed
- a weather vane to show which way the wind blows
- a rain gauge to show how much rain falls

Some of these tools are complex, so if you build a station, you and your family may need to buy them. But it's easy to make your own weather vane and rain gauge. Here's how.

MAKE A RAIN GAUGE

You'll need:

- a clear glass jar, with no label, at least two inches (5 cm) tall
- tape—masking or duct tape is easier to write on
- a ruler
- a funnel with an opening at least the same size as the base of the jar

1 Place a strip of tape along the full height of the glass jar. Stand the ruler alongside the tape and mark off inches and half inches. Make the lines longer for the inches so you can easily tell the two measurements apart.

2 Place the funnel in the jar.

3 Before it rains, place your gauge outside. Bring it inside when the rain stops to see how much fell. Empty the gauge before the next rainstorm.

MAKE A WEATHER VANE

You'll need:

- a pencil with an eraser
- cardboard
- scissors
- tape
- a straw
- a pin
- a ball of clay about 1.5 inches (4 cm) in diameter
- a compass

1. Using the pencil, draw the shape of the pointer and tail for your wind arrow on the cardboard, then cut them out. Tape one to each end of the straw.

2. Place your straw arrow horizontally on top of the eraser and hold it in place there with the pin. Make sure the arrow can spin freely.

3. Place the clay on a flat surface outside and stand the pencil in it.

4. Place the compass near your weather vane. The arrow will point in the direction the wind is coming from. If the arrow points east, the wind is blowing from the east toward the west.

Working With WEATHER

WEATHERCASTER AL ROKER

A METEOROLOGIST AT WORK

Are you wowed by weather, watching the skies, pouring over forecasts, or taking measurements from your own weather station? Then you might want to consider a career as a meteorologist, climatologist, or other weather-watcher, like some of the people you've met in this book.

FIRST STEPS

To work with weather, you'll most likely need a college degree. And you'll want to take lots of math and science courses, which you can start doing while you're in high school. Knowing the ins and outs of computers is good, too, because weather scientists rely on them to do their job. Dozens of colleges and universities in North America offer degrees in meteorology and related fields. Many also offer advanced degrees, beyond the usual four-year program.

Outside of school, you can see if there is a meteorological club near you. The American Meteorological Society sponsors clubs across the United States. These clubs are mostly for college students and people working in the field, but many take part in events open to the public. You can also look for science fairs that seek projects related to meteorology. One sponsored by NOAA, the GOES Virtual Science Fair, accepts projects from middle school and high school students.

GET TO WORK!

With a degree in hand, college graduates can opt for a number of career paths. An obvious place to start is the National Weather Service. More than half its 4,600 workers are meteorologists. If you like the idea of being in front of an audience, you could deliver the forecast on radio or TV stations. Note: Not all weather people on TV are meteorologists! Some simply deliver the weather information prepared for them by forecasters and meteorologists.

Meteorologists are also needed by

- the military, especially in the U.S. Navy and Air Force;
- airlines, to help planes avoid bad weather;
- universities, to teach the next generation of weather and climate scientists; and
- the legal field, which relies on special meteorologists to provide weather data related to court cases.

Some meteorologists become consultants. That means they work independently and are hired by private companies that need detailed weather data but can't afford to pay for a full-time meteorologist.

BOLD IN THE COLD

You can pursue a weather-related career without being a meteorologist. Randy Julander studied hydrology, the science of water, before he took a job with the U.S. Department of Agriculture. Now, he studies water in a frozen form—snow. Whether going by ski, snowmobile, or helicopter, Julander and his team head to snowy mountain peaks. There, they measure snow depth, precipitation, temperature, and other factors. The information they gather helps people know how much snowmelt they can expect when summer comes. Too little, and the odds increase for a bad wildfire season. Too much, and floods could be on the way.

The weather biz is hoppin'!

NOAA DOPPLER RADAR STATION, TAMPA, FLORIDA, U.S.A.

Weather
WHIZ QUIZ

Are you a weather whiz? Prove it, with a weather quiz! See how much you remember about weather, climate, and natural disasters.

All three of Earth's tropical climate zones have only two basic seasons: wet and dry.

FALSE!

The savanna, one of the tropical zones, has three seasons: One is cool and dry, one is hot and dry, and the third is hot and wet.

The Johnstown Flood of 1889 marked the first time the American Red Cross helped survivors of a natural disaster.

TRUE!

The American Red Cross was created just eight years before that massive flood in Pennsylvania, by a nurse named Clara Barton. The flood destroyed large parts of the town.

The Fujita scale is used to describe the strength of hurricanes.

FALSE!

The Fujita scale indicates the destructive power of tornadoes, based on their wind speed and how much damage they cause. Hurricanes are rated from Category 1 to 5, based on wind speed, on the Saffir-Simpson scale.

You can use thunder to tell how far away you are from a lightning bolt.

TRUE!

Light and sound work together to help you make that calculation. After a lightning flash, the number of seconds that pass before a thunderclap tell you how far away the lightning is. If it takes five seconds, the lightning is about one mile (1.6 km) away. If the thunder comes after just one second, the lightning is only about 1,000 feet (305 m) away.

An anemometer is used to measure air pressure.

FALSE!

An anemometer measures wind speed. A barometer measures air pressure, with rising pressure signaling fair weather is on the way.

Greenhouse gases are what farmers use to grow crops indoors.

FALSE!

Greenhouse gases are gases that trap heat in the atmosphere, creating global warming. Between 1990 and 2015, human activity caused the amount of greenhouse gases in the atmosphere to increase by 43 percent.

Thanks to the water cycle, rain that falls today could be billions of years old.

TRUE!

With help from the sun, water is constantly on the move, going from sources on the ground into the sky, then falling back to Earth as precipitation.

Zephyr, a kind of wind, is named for a Greek god.

TRUE!

To the ancient Greeks, Zephyr was the god of the west wind, and that word is still used today to describe a gentle breeze.

Asia, home to the Himalaya and other mountain ranges, has the highest average elevation of the seven continents.

FALSE!

The cold, hard fact is that Antarctica's thick layers of ice make it the continent with the highest average elevation of the seven continents—about 8,200 feet (2,500 m).

GLOSSARY

ACCUMULATION
The amount of rain, snow, or ice that builds on solid surfaces

AMOC
Atlantic Meridional Overturning Circulation, a system of currents that move warm and cold water in the Atlantic Ocean

ATMOSPHERE
Gases and tiny, solid particles surrounding Earth and extending thousands of miles into space

BRUMATION
A form of dormancy that some reptiles and amphibians enter during winter

CLIMATOLOGIST
A scientist who studies Earth's climate

CRYOSPHERE
The total of all frozen water on Earth

DERECHO
A widespread, long-lasting windstorm associated with severe thunderstorms

DORMANCY
A state of inactivity many animals enter during winter

DROPLET
A tiny drop of a liquid

EURASIAN
Describing the combined landmass of Europe and Asia

EVACUATE
To leave an area facing the threat of a natural disaster

EVAPORATION
When a liquid changes to a gas

EYEWALL
The part of a hurricane surrounding its eye, or center, where the strongest winds occur

FLOE
A sheet of floating ice

FOSSIL FUELS
Fuels formed from the decayed remains of ancient wildlife and plants

GLACIER
A slow-moving mass of ice

GREENHOUSE GASES
Gases in the atmosphere that trap heat, keeping it close to Earth's surface

GULF STREAM
A warm ocean current that starts in the Gulf of Mexico and moves toward northern Europe

HABOOB
A powerful dust storm

HEAT INDEX
The combined effect of temperature and humidity on human skin

HIBERNATION
A state of dormancy for some animals marked by falling body temperatures and slowed heartbeat and metabolism

ICE SHEET
Permanent layer of ice covering a large area of land

INDIGENOUS
Describing someone or something native to a particular area

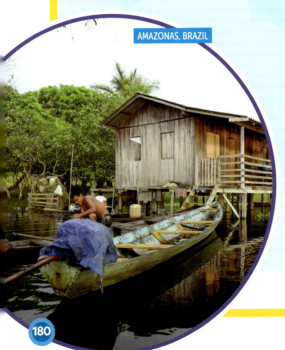
AMAZONAS, BRAZIL

INFRASOUND
A sound too low in frequency for humans to hear

INTERNAL CLIMATE MIGRATION
The movement of people within one country because of global warming

KATABATIC
Referring to winds that blow down a slope

METEOROLOGICAL
Relating to meteorology, the study of the atmosphere and how changes in it affect weather

MICROCLIMATE
A small region with a climate different from the areas around it

MIGRATE
To move from one place to another

ORGANIC
Relating to living matter

PARTS PER MILLION
A measurement that indicates the percentage of small amounts of a given material in a much larger substance

PERMAFROST
Permanently frozen layer of soil

POLAR VORTEX
A large area of cold air and low pressure near the North and South Poles

PRECIPITATION
Water that falls from clouds as either a liquid or solid

STORM CLOUDS

REFRACTION
The bending of light waves as they pass from one substance to another

SPOTTING
The spreading of a wildfire created by winds carrying burning embers

STORM SURGE
The water pushed ashore by a hurricane's winds

SUPERCELL
A severe thunderstorm that can produce high wind, large hail, and tornadoes

TRANSPIRATION
The evaporation of water in plants

TROPICAL
Referring to the region around the Equator from 23.5° north latitude to 23.5° south latitude

UPDRAFT
An upward movement of air

VAPOR
Matter, like water, that is in a gaseous state

WATER CYCLE
The constant movement of Earth's water from the ground to the clouds and back, fueled by the sun's energy

WINDCHILL
The combined effect of cold temperature and wind speed on human skin

SVALBARD GLOBAL SEED VAULT, NORWAY

INDEX

Boldface indicates illustrations.

INDEX

PHOTO CREDITS